LEARN CHESS
IN A WEEKEND

LEARN CHESS
IN A WEEKEND

KEN WHYLD

Photography by Philip Gatward

ALFRED A. KNOPF
New York
1993

A DORLING KINDERSLEY BOOK

This edition is a Borzoi Book, published in 1993 by Alfred A. Knopf, Inc.,
by arrangement with Dorling Kindersley.

Art Editor Kevin Williams
Project Editor Liz Wheeler
Series Art Editor Amanda Lunn
Series Editor Jo Weeks
Managing Art Editor Tina Vaughan
Managing Editor Sean Moore
Production Controller Helen Creeke

Library of Congress Cataloging-in-Publication Data

Whyld, Ken
  Learn Chess in a Weekend / by Ken Whyld. -- 1st ed.
      p. cm. -- (Learn in a weekend series)
  Includes index.
  ISBN 0-679-42229-3 :
  1. Chess. I. Title. II. Series
GV1448.W47   1993   92-54793
                                         CIP

Computer page make-up by
Cloud 9 Designs, Hampshire, and
Book Production Services, Norfolk
Reproduced by Colourscan, Singapore
Printed in Italy by
Arnoldo Mondadori, Verona

First American Edition

CONTENTS

Introduction 6

PREPARING FOR THE WEEKEND 8

THE WEEKEND COURSE 20

Day 1

Day 2

AFTER THE WEEKEND 84

INTRODUCTION

CHESS IN A WEEKEND – is it possible? The game of kings has fascinated generals and foot soldiers, scientists and laborers, empresses and maids, for about 1400 years, and yet nobody has been able to play it perfectly. However, you will learn to play a game in a weekend. Indeed, you will be able to play even before the halfway stage. By then you will have been told absolutely everything you need to know, and nothing that is not essential. If you have some idea of the game already, you are still urged to work through the full weekend program, even if you spend less time on the earlier skills than we have allowed – you may find that there are gaps in your knowledge. At the conclusion of the weekend you will be able to play a reasonable game. Then you can decide how strong you want

WOMEN'S CHESS CHAMPION
Ken Whyld is seen here enjoying a challenging game with Cathy Forbes, who first won the British Women's Championship at the age of 19. Cathy has gone on to represent her country in the Chess Olympiads, and carries the title of Women's International Master.

to be, and how much time you are willing to invest in reaching that level. If you are in no hurry, you could split your weekend. After day one, break off and play a number of games. In this way you will consolidate your knowledge of the movement of the chessmen, and at the same time become aware of areas that need improvement. Then look to day two for guidance. Only by playing games can you expect to become strong. Book study speeds the process. Part of the magic of chess is its inexhaustibility. Potentially there are more different games of chess than there are atoms in the universe, so you need have no fear of getting in a rut. A famous chess player, Siegbert Tarrasch, said "Chess, like love, like music, has the power to make men happy". That must be good value for a few hours of your time.

Ken Whyld.

KEN WHYLD

PREPARING FOR THE WEEKEND

Making a success of your weekend with some preparation

MAKING YOURSELF READY for the weekend will give you some practice in one of the skills developed by playing chess – foresight. You will need to equip yourself with a chess set. There are sets to meet every budget, and you will not necessarily do better by spending more. Even if you already have some idea of the game, do be prepared to start at the beginning, as your knowledge may be incomplete. Once you can play, you will want to have as many games as you can, and improve your proficiency. Ideally, you

A relatively cheap Staunton set

Older chessmen are often ornate

A small computer is ideal for travelling

THE RIGHT EQUIPMENT

Be practical in your choice of equipment. Match your budget and your space to the set you buy (see pp.10-11). Only Staunton pattern (opposite) will do, and your board should be in the right proportion for the men. A luxurious set will not improve your play. Beautiful sets like this one, left, are too fragile for use.

THE ORIGINS OF THE GAME

Knowing that chess began in ancient times as an imitation of warfare will help you to understand the purpose of the game (see pp.12-13). It is important not to lose sight of the aim of play. Chess has a rich and fascinating history, which you may wish to pursue later.

should play with someone stronger than yourself if you want to progress, but such a person is not always ready and willing! An ideal alternative is the chess computer – it never says no. Those designed for beginners are best, because they have special facilities to help the novice, and they are relatively cheap. Some are pocket size, and are useful for someone who wants to play while travelling. Others provide a standard board, and so can also be used for conventional games between two players. It will help if you can be free from interruptions during your weekend, especially on day one when you are laying the foundations. Once you have mastered the basics, you will never forget them. Words in **bold** throughout this book are given further explanation in the glossary (pp.92-93).

STAUNTON MEN
Your set will be of this pattern, although size, amount of detail, and weight may vary compared with the ones we show (see pp.16-17). Before the weekend, learn to recognize each **piece** and the pawns, to proceed quickly into a study of their movements.

THE BOARD
Learn the conventional terms used to describe features of the board, and also how to set it up correctly (see pp.14-15). Even before you know how to play you will be able to spot the many instances in movies where the board's orientation is wrong, although never in movies starring Humphrey Bogart, as he was a skillful chess player!

SETTING UP THE MEN
You can easily reveal your lack of experience if you are slow as you set up the **pieces** – or even worse, use the wrong squares! Every game you play calls on you to place the men correctly on their starting squares – the **array**. Learn how to do this from the step-by-step guide (see pp.18-19).

Stage four – nearly a full rank

Stage two – two pairs have been placed

All of the black team in their array

WHAT YOU NEED

All the king's horses and all the king's men

YOU NEED A BOARD AND CHESSMEN. Choose carefully. Boards are usually classified by the size of their squares. If the squares are less than about 2.5cm (1in) you may find it hard to grasp the men. If the board is too large, you may have to stretch when playing. The most popular square size is 5cm (2in). Black and white squares are tiring on the eyes, so select brown, or green, with cream. Materials range from cheap folding card or vinyl roll-up boards, to crafted inlaid wood.

PROPORTIONS

Sets are usually described by the height of the kings, the tallest men in most sets. Match the size of the men to the squares of the board, right. The diameter of the base of the largest piece should be about three-quarters the width of the squares.

¹/₈ square on both sides

10cm (4in)

5cm (2in)

SOLID BOARD
Pick a size that suits the table you will use most often. Try to have a stable base – boards can have a nasty habit of being "accidentally" knocked over when a player is near to defeat!

CHESSMEN
Insist on Staunton pattern chessmen, as shown throughout this book. These are recognized throughout the world, and you cannot expect your opponent to be familiar with other shapes.

• HEAVY MEN
These men are weighted, to give them stability.

FOR THE PRICE OF THIS BOOK

A set with kings of 9-10cm (3$^1/_2$-4in) in height goes well on a board with 5cm (2in) squares. Such a combination should cost anything between the price of this book, for a card board and plastic men (below), up to ten times as much for a good wooden set and board (below left).

• FOLDING CENTER
This card chess board folds in the center for easy storage when not in use.

PLASTIC •
Good quality plastic men are often more pleasing than similarly priced wooden sets.

CHESS COMPUTERS

For the price of a better set you can buy a chess computer, and most will include men. An elementary computer is highly recommended to improve your play. Don't go for a top-of-the-range model designed to challenge a champion, as these are stronger than more than 99% of players. There are also programs available for use on many personal computers.

• SET OF MEN
The men in this set activate a pressure-sensitive chessboard.

BASIC MODEL

A machine designed for beginners will not only be relatively cheap, it will have features that are invaluable to the novice. By the time you can beat your computer regularly there will be improved machines available at the higher levels.

TWO-DIMENSIONAL MEN •
The cheapest computers have two-dimensional chessmen, for you to plot your moves on the mini board.

WHAT IS CHESS?

The nature of the game

CHESS WAS CREATED as an imitation of warfare. The sole aim is to capture the opponent's king, and any hardship or sacrifice is worthwhile if that end is achieved. The game originated in an age of despotic rulers when it was wise not to offend monarchs, so the king is never actually taken, and the game ends if his capture cannot be avoided on the next move. The queen and the bishop are relatively recent arrivals on the battlefield, having replaced a counselor and an elephant respectively. The game began in the East, where elephants were used in military campaigns. The other elements were foot soldiers (pawns), cavalry (knights), and chariots (rooks).

19TH CENTURY SET
This oriental set was carved in the 19th century, for the European market. The battle allegory is clear in these ferocious figures.

KING •
The king has always been the most important **piece** and often the tallest.

ROOK •
Rukh in Arabic means chariot. Now the **piece** is represented by a tower.

QUEEN •
The queen has now replaced the counselor at the king's side on the chess battlefield.

BATTLE ON BOARD

Chess is played on a board of 64 squares between two players – one known as White, the other Black. Each team has 16 chessmen. Both sides have exactly the same number and type of men. There is no element of chance, as everything can be seen. White begins the game by making one move, then Black replies, and so on until the game ends in victory for one player, or in a draw.

KNIGHT •
All the chessmen were professional soldiers at one time. The knight remains the most identifiable.

• BISHOP
Throughout the world the identity of this **piece** varies. Here it is a cleric.

• PAWN
In comparison to today's pawns, these foot soldiers look quite fierce.

THE BOARD

The scene of the battle takes place on the board

YOU MAY LIKE TO THINK of the chessboard as a battleground,
or perhaps as an artist's canvas on which you will create great
masterpieces. After you have had a few bruising encounters, you
may begin to feel it is more like the arena of a streetfight, or the
annual sale at a department store. Whatever your vision, you
need to become thoroughly familiar with each of the 64 squares.
You will find, as you become more expert, that the squares nearest
the middle of the board are often the location of the most
interesting action, but you must never become so hypnotized that
you fail to keep an eye on the whole board. After a little practice
you will find it easier to see the board as a whole – beginners
can often suffer from tunnel vision.

ORIENTATION

The board must be placed so that on
the first row, each player's right-hand
corner square is white. The nature of
the game is not changed if the board is
placed the other way, but the laws of
chess lay down this convention.

WHITE'S RIGHT
Remember which way to
place the board with the
phrase, "white on the
right", so that a white
square is always in the
right corner of the **rank**.

• BLACK SQUARES
The dark squares are usually referred to
as "black", although they seldom are.

LIGHT SQUARES •
The light squares are
usually called "white".

THE ROWS

The rows of alternate colored squares running from left to right are **ranks**, and the rows from one player's side to the other are **files**. To remember which is which, think of your men as army ranks.

RANKS •
There are eight **ranks**, and each row has eight squares.

• **FILES**
There are also eight **files**, each of eight squares.

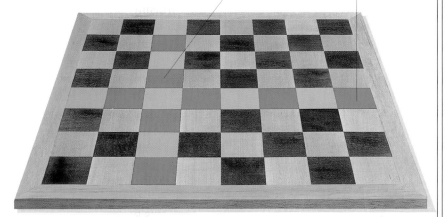

DIAGONALS
The third kind of row on the chessboard is the **diagonal**. In each case the squares are all the same color. There are four diagonals, two all-white and two all-black, with each of two, three, four, five, six, and seven squares. However, there are only two diagonals – one white and one black – with eight squares.

• **COUNT THE DIAGONALS**
Check for yourself. It may seem strange that while there are only eight **ranks** and eight **files**, there are 26 distinct **diagonals**.

TWO DIAGONALS •
From here, there is one **diagonal** of six squares to the right (in green), and one of three to the left.

LONG DIAGONAL •
The longest **diagonals** on the board have eight squares.

THE CHESSMEN

Recognizing the pawns and **pieces**

A LEADING ENGLISH PLAYER of the mid-19th century, Howard Staunton, worked tirelessly to forge agreement throughout the world on such matters as the uniformity of the rules of chess. He urged that only one of the many styles of men in use at the time be retained, and he influenced the design, which is illustrated throughout this book. Staunton pattern chessmen are named after him, and are the only ones allowed in competition throughout the world. Each side has 16 chessmen, of six different shapes. Eight of these are identical – they are the pawns. The other eight are called **pieces**. It is not strictly correct to refer to pawns as pieces, although it often happens.

THE PIECES

Each side has two single **pieces** – the king and queen. While the king is the most important piece, it is far from being the most powerful. The queen is the most potent. Pairs of bishops, knights, and rooks complete the team of pieces.

• THE KING
The king is usually the tallest chesspiece, as befits his authority.

• THE QUEEN
The queen is identified by her crown.

• THE BISHOP
The top of the bishop is said to resemble a bishop's miter.

ORNAMENTAL CHESS SETS

The earliest chessmen known are very simple, dating from the period when Islam dominated chess. The Koran outlawed the representation of living figures, human or animal. Since the Renaissance there have been a great many beautifully crafted sets, although frequently they are too precious, too fragile, or too confusing to use in play. This set is evocative of men in battle, but is too delicate for routine games.

• **BISHOP**
The white bishop wears traditional clerical robes and carries a staff.

KNIGHT •
This knight shows the soldier as well as his horse.

• **ROYAL PAIR**
This king and queen are intended to be likenesses of Napoleon and Josephine.

ROOK •
This rook shows a standard bearer on a fortress tower, with a fragile pennon.

• **PAWN**
The white pawn differs from the red pawn of the same set (see pp.12-13).

• **THE KNIGHT**
A horse's head represents the only piece that jumps.

• **THE PAWN**
The pawns are the most simply designed of all the men.

• **THE ROOK**
The rook looks like a castle, and nonplayers sometimes incorrectly use that name.

PLACING THE MEN

"Put the right man in the right place" – Schiller

REMEMBER "WHITE ON THE RIGHT" before you place the men on the board. All the pieces stand on the **rank** nearest their player. In some expensive sets one knight and rook on each side are stamped with a crown, and these should begin in the king's half of the board.

CORNERSTONES
The cornerstones of the **array** are the rooks, one at each end of the **rank**, like towers in a fortress. As with all the pairs, one begins on dark squares, one on light.

FOUR SQUARE •
Place one rook in each corner of the first **rank**.

NEXT COME THE KNIGHTS
The knights stand on the first **rank**, next to the rooks. Of all the chess **pieces** these look the most directional, but whichever way they are facing has no effect on their power.

CROWN STAMP •
Place the crown-stamped knight on the **king's side**.

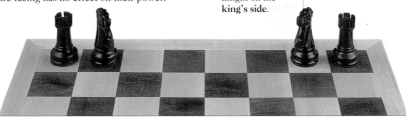

FLANKING THE ROYAL PAIR
The bishops stand next to the knights, nearest the center of the board. The bishop, king, and queen all have similar pedestals, but their heads have different shapes.

• **SLOTTED HEAD**
The slotted head of the bishop could be said to resemble a miter.

QUEEN ON HER COLOR
There are two empty central squares left on this **rank**, and the queen stands on the one that is her color. The usual way to remember this is, "the queen takes her own color".

• BLACK QUEEN
The black queen is placed on the central black square, facing the white queen on the same **file**.

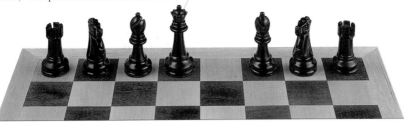

KINGS FACING
The king stands on the remaining central square. From White's side of the board, the queen is to the left of the king, and from Black's side, the queen is to the right.

• KING'S HEAD
The king is usually the tallest **piece**, distinguished by the cross on its top.

THE SECOND RANK
The second **rank** is full of pawns, one in front of each **piece**. Although they are all the same in appearance, you will soon learn that there is a hierarchy among them.

• CENTRAL PAWNS
Those pawns "born" nearest the center are likely to be more powerful in "life".

READY TO PLAY
This is the board set up in the initial **array**, before the game commences. Black and White mirror each other. In most Staunton pattern sets the **pieces** step down in physical size from king, or queen, to rook. Keep all this in mind to avoid the telltale signs of a beginner, such as placing the board the wrong way round, or the queens on the wrong squares.

THE WEEKEND COURSE

Understanding the course at a glance

THE COURSE COVERS FIFTEEN BASIC SKILLS in two days. After Skill 6 on the first day, you will have learned everything you need in order to be able to play chess correctly. If you like, you can break off at this stage and play a few games against someone who knows the game, or even better, against a computer. You will then find that there is a huge difference between being able to play and being able to win. After that the focus is on learning to play more skillfully, and generally refining and improving your game.

Black king

King

Knight

White knight

DAY 1		Hours	Page
SKILL 1	Line pieces	¾	22-27
SKILL 2	The knight	½	28-31
SKILL 3	The king	½	32-35
SKILL 4	The pawn	¾	36-41
SKILL 5	Check	¾	42-45
SKILL 6	Draw	¾	46-47
SKILL 7	Scores	1	48-49
SKILL 8	Play	1	50-53

KEY TO SYMBOLS

CLOCKS
The clocks indicate how long you might like to spend on each skill, and where it fits into your 6-hour day. The blue segment in the clock on p.28 shows ½ hour is set aside for Skill 2; the grey shaded area shows you have already spent ¾ hour learning Skill 1.

**RATING SYSTEM ••••• **
Each skill is rated according to its degree of difficulty. Two bullets (••) denote the skill is comparatively easy. Five bullets indicate a more challenging skill, which may need more practice after the weekend.

THE BOARDS
Squares that are colored green on the chessboards show the men's direction of travel, and red denotes a capture. You will find acquiring these skills a great deal easier if your standard chess set is at your side to help you follow the course. Play through all the exercises and games featured, so that you can clearly see all the implications of each move. You will miss many subtleties if you try to play along in your head.

Model boards help you through the course

Quizzes are shown on a traditional board

White queen

DAY 2		Hours	Page
SKILL 9	Material	¾	54-57
SKILL 10	Opening	1	58-61
SKILL 11	Tactics	1¼	62-67
SKILL 12	Strategy	¾	68-71
SKILL 13	Endgame	¾	72-75
SKILL 14	Handling pawns	¾	76-79
SKILL 15	Best moves	¾	80-81

A rook is worth five pawns

A knight and a bishop are each worth three pawns

LINE PIECES

Definition: *The moves of the rook, the bishop, and the queen*

LINE PIECES ARE THOSE THAT MOVE in straight lines over any number of available squares. You will remember from your study of the board (pp.14-15) that it has **diagonal** rows, where squares join at the corners, and two kinds of orthogonal rows – **ranks** and **files** – where squares link at the sides, giving three kinds of straight line.

OBJECTIVE: To learn how to handle the rook, bishop, and queen. *Rating* ••

THE ROOK

The rook is the simplest of line pieces, moving along ranks or files

SCOPE OF MOVE

The rook can move any distance in either direction on the **rank** or **file** on which it stands, until it reaches an occupied square. Empty your board, place a rook on its starting square, and count how many squares are available to it. Now try this from several other squares. Unlike other **pieces**, the rook has the same range on any square.

CROWN STAMP
The crown stamp on this rook identifies it as beginning on the **king's side** rather than the **queen's side** in a game.

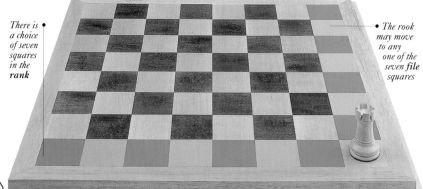

There is a choice of seven squares in the **rank**

• The rook may move to any one of the seven **file** squares

BLOCKED PATH

A rook may not move beyond an occupied square, or onto one on which one of its own side stands. In this position, right, the rook can move four squares forward, or three backwards, or three to the right, or two to the left. It is blocked by the white knight, so here the rook controls 12 squares.

TEAM-MATE •
The rook's team-mate blocks its path, leaving only two available squares to the left instead of four.

• FILE CONTROL
The rook has complete freedom on the **file**, and controls all the squares.

ROOK ATTACKING

If an enemy man stands in its path, the rook may capture it by going onto that square and removing the enemy from the board. In this position the rook has an additional square available to it.

• THE SAME RANK
The white rook can attack the black knight, as it stands on the same **rank**.

• TAKEN PLACE
The rook takes the knight's square, as it is removed from the board.

The knight

QUIZ BOX

Where can the white rook move if it is White's turn to play? If it is Black's turn, where can the black rook move? How many squares are available to each?

It is the same figure, ten, for each of them. If White takes the knight, how does that alter the squares controlled by the black rook? It can go one square further, and take the white rook.

SKILL 1 THE BISHOP

After the rook, the bishop's move is the next simplest to learn

BISHOP'S SCOPE

Like the rook, the bishop can move in straight lines until it meets an obstruction, and if that is an enemy, the bishop can capture it. Unlike the rook, the bishop moves **diagonally**. One bishop from each side moves only on dark squares, and the other only on light.

WHITE ELEPHANT
Above: The elephant **piece** preceded the bishop on the chess battlefield. This is an 18th-century Burmese piece.

• DARK SQUARES
A bishop on this square can travel to any of these highlighted dark squares, and can only capture enemies on dark squares.

BISHOP'S RANGE
This bishop can only ever reach the 32 dark squares, and can never meet its team-mate on the light squares. In play, two bishops are rated as more than twice the worth of one.

BISHOP'S POTENCY
This chart shows the bishop's range across the whole board. With the bishop in its starting place, count how many squares it covers. Move it forward one square, and count again. From the bishop's starting square next to the king, count how many moves you need to reach the square where the enemy king begins the game. How many ways are there of doing this in two moves? How many in three? Did you find five?

7	7	7	7	7	7	7	7
7	9	9	9	9	9	9	7
7	9	11	11	11	11	9	7
7	9	11	13	13	11	9	7
7	9	11	13	13	11	9	7
7	9	11	11	11	11	9	7
7	9	9	9	9	9	9	7
7	7	7	7	7	7	7	7

• POTENTIAL
The blue figures represent the number of squares to which the bishop could move.

• CENTER
The bishop is more mobile nearer the center of the board, unlike the rook, which is the same.

WHITE BISHOP •
The white bishop can only move to eight squares.

• WHITE ROOK
The rook's movement on the **ranks** or **files** is not hindered by its team-mate.

BLOCKED PATH

In the position left, the bishop can move to either of the two squares up and left, or the two down and left. It could also move to any of the four squares up right, but it cannot move down and to the right because its own team-mate obstructs that direction completely.

BISHOP ATTACKING

Here the bishop has all the possibilities it had in the position above, but this time it can also move down and right one square, taking the enemy rook. The bishop captures in exactly the same manner as the rook, displacing the enemy from its square and the game.

WHITE BISHOP •
Taking the rook increases the bishop's range.

• BLACK ROOK
The black rook is not attacking the white bishop.

DISPLACEMENT

To complete the move, the bishop takes the black rook's square. In all chess **piece** captures, the attacker takes the place of the victim.

The rook

QUIZ BOX

If it is White's turn to play, where can the white bishop move? Where can the black bishop move if it is Black's turn?

Did you reach nine for White, and five for Black? If White moves first and captures the knight, does that alter the number of squares controlled by the black bishop? Can Black recapture, by taking the white bishop?

THE QUEEN

*The queen moves on **ranks**, **files**,
or **diagonals***

THE QUEEN'S REIGN

Now that you can move the rook and
the bishop, the queen is easy. On any
one move it moves like a rook, or like
a bishop. However, the queen can
never move as a mixture of both of
them. In the male-oriented world of
chess, the queen is boss. No other
piece can face it on equal terms.

COUNSELOR
Above: The queen is
relatively new. In this
18th-century Burmese
set there is a counselor
instead, with his king.

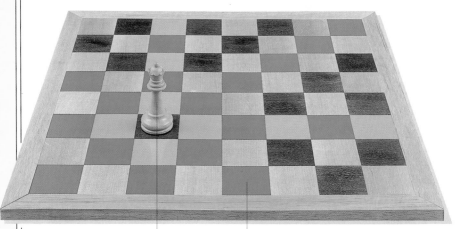

RANKS AND FILES •
Like the rook, the queen
can move along the
ranks and **files**, but it
has additional powers.

• DIAGONALS
Like the bishop, the queen can
move along the **diagonals**. The
combined process gives the
queen great range and speed.

QUEEN'S POTENCY
This is the potency chart for the
queen, showing the number of
squares available to it, from each
square on an empty board. As you
might expect, the number of squares
covered by a queen on an open board
is the 14 the rook would cover, plus
the 7 to 13 that a bishop would cover
on the same square. The queen is the
most powerful **piece** on the board,
and a great favorite with beginners
who like the way it can hurtle around.

21	21	21	21	21	21	21	21
21	23	23	23	23	23	23	21
21	23	25	25	25	25	23	21
21	23	25	27	27	25	23	21
21	23	25	27	27	25	23	21
21	23	25	25	25	25	23	21
21	23	23	23	23	23	23	21
21	21	21	21	21	21	21	21

• EDGE
A queen has
reduced powers
when on one of
the border squares
of the board.

• CENTER
Every step nearer
the center of the
board adds two
squares to the
queen's range.

ROYAL COMMAND

Find out how many squares are available to the queen here. If the square on which the black bishop stands is included, you should have counted 23 squares. Here, the queen does not have 25 squares available to it, as shown on the chart at the foot of the page opposite. This is because the queen is unable to go to any of the squares that are beyond the enemy **piece**.

• **BLACK BISHOP**
The bishop is not in a position to threaten the queen, nor can it move to do so.

• **WHITE QUEEN**
The queen takes the bishop's place, after it has been captured and removed from the board.

The bishop

QUIZ BOX

Where can the queen go? Which captures can it make? If Black moves first, which moves or captures are available? What if Black's rook and bishop change places?

If White moves first, the queen can take either the rook or the bishop. Taking the rook is best, not only because it is worth more than the bishop (see pp.54-57), but also because it is undefended. The rook defends the bishop, being on the same **rank**. If Black has first move, neither of its **pieces** is presently attacking the queen. If the bishop and the rook swapped places, they would both be threatening it.

SKILL

2 THE KNIGHT

DAY 1

Definition: *How the knight moves and captures*

AFTER THE SIMPLICITY of the line **pieces** the knight's move comes as something of a shock, but the piece gives a great deal of joy, as well was a few unpleasant surprises, to those learning to play. Unlike any other chessman it leaves one square and arrives on another without having been anywhere in between, as if in a time-travel science fiction story. In other words, it has no fixed path.

OBJECTIVE: To master the knight. *Rating* • • • •

KNIGHT MOVES

Much the best way to learn how the knight moves is to study the board below. This gives you a clear vision of the squares available to it. Like the other **pieces** examined, the knight captures by displacing an enemy man on a square to which it could have moved, had that square been vacant.

HORSE'S HEAD
From the beginning of chess, this **piece** has always represented a soldier on horseback.

ARRIVAL SQUARE •
This is one of eight possible arrival squares available to this knight on a central square.

• NO PATHWAY
Unlike the line **pieces**, the knight has no fixed path, and can "leap over" pieces en route to its destination.

KNIGHT BLOCKED

Now study this board. The knight has one less square available to it. The presence of a queen from the same team on one of the squares reduces the moves. It is never possible to take an ally, although sometimes it would be helpful if it was. Note that the knight does not block the queen's path.

MOVING KNIGHT •
This time only seven squares are highlighted as potential destinations for the knight.

• QUEEN ALLY
The knight cannot move onto the queen's square.

KNIGHT ATTACK

Now consider this position. It is similar, but the queen is a foe so the knight has eight squares available. Note that if a knight moves, it no longer maintains any threats or defenses from its previous position.

ATTACKED QUEEN •
If the knight moves to another square, the queen will no longer be under attack. The queen cannot attack the knight.

• WHITE KNIGHT
The knight has moved onto the queen's square and taken her.

The queen

HOW THE KNIGHT MOVES

Everybody has their own favorite way of remembering the knight's move. The best ones do not trace a fixed route, because this kind of visualization can lead to mistakes. Here are some hints, in no particular sequence. Pick the one that suits you, and then forget the others. Remember that the knight cannot be blocked en route, only by an ally on an arrival square. The knight moves:
• To the next-but-one square of the opposite color to its starting square.

• To the nearest square that a queen couldn't reach from the same position.
• To the diagonally opposite corner of a rectangle of 2 by 3 squares.
• One square forward or sideways and then one diagonally continuing away from the departure square.
• Two squares forward and then one sideways, at right angles.
• One square diagonally and then one forward or sideways, continuing away from the departure square.

SKILL
2 KNIGHT ATTACK

The knight is on the same starting square as before (pp.28-29), with White to move. Count how many options the knight has now. If there was any hesitation before you saw that it could capture the black rook, it might be because you are tracing the route. Go back a page until you are confident you have a clear picture.

ENEMY ROOK •
The black rook is threatened by the white knight, but not by any other piece.

The rook

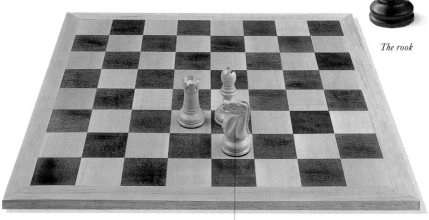

SOLE AGGRESSOR
The black rook was not threatened by the white bishop, which was on the same **file** but can only move **diagonally**, or by the white rook, which can only move orthogonally.

• ROOK'S POSITION
The white knight has taken the black rook's place on the board. The other white **pieces** did not obstruct the knight's ability to capture.

KNIGHT POWER
This chart shows the number of squares available to a knight on an empty board. Find the least moves a knight takes from your king's starting square to the enemy queen's, and then try a few less direct routes. It is always an even number of moves. The route from king to king always takes an odd number. Any other **piece** can perhaps make a waiting move, and maintain its attack or defense; a knight cannot. This knowledge will be vital to you as you improve.

2	3	4	4	4	4	3	2
3	4	6	6	6	6	4	3
4	6	8	8	8	8	6	4
4	6	8	8	8	8	6	4
4	6	8	8	8	8	6	4
4	6	8	8	8	8	6	4
3	4	6	6	6	6	4	3
2	3	4	4	4	4	3	2

• 2-SQUARE
A knight in a "2-square" that is preventing **mate** is worth more than one in an "8-square" doing nothing.

• 6-SQUARE
A knight firmly established on a "6-square" in the enemy camp may be worth more than one on an "8-square".

BLACK BISHOP •
The black bishop is under attack from all of the white **pieces**, but it could capture the white bishop if Black has first move.

The bishop

JOINT ATTACK

This position looks similar to that shown opposite. However, White can now capture the bishop in three ways. If Black is to move first, it can only attack the bishop. Remember that if a knight threatens a foe other than a knight, that man can never be threatening the knight in return.

WHITE KNIGHT •
The white knight takes the black bishop, and goes from an "8-square" to a "6-square".

QUIZ BOX

QUIZ 1
If White has the first move, where can the knight go? Which captures could it make? If Black has first move, how many squares and captures are available to its knight?

QUIZ 2
White's knight has just moved. Which men are attacked? How many squares can the knight reach from this square? Can Black capture the knight?

White can make two captures to Black's none

Black can capture the knight, which attacks three men

SKILL

3

THE KING

Definition: *The powers of the king*

YOU ALREADY KNOW that the king is the most important **piece** in the game. Any other piece can disappear and the game goes on, but once the king is overpowered the game is over. You might therefore expect it to have ferocious strength. The opposite is the case. The king needs sheltering for much of the game, and usually only joins in the battle when few men are left on the board.

OBJECTIVE: To learn the king's moves, including **castling**. *Rating* • • • •

STATELY MOVE

In many ways, the king's move is the easiest to describe. The king moves, or captures, one square only in any direction. Although that might sound simple, there are two additional special considerations that are explored in this skill.

KING'S SPECIALITY
The first of the king's two distinguishing features is this: as the aim of the game is to capture the enemy king, a king can never move to a square on which it could be captured, that is, move into **check**. This means, for example, that the two kings can never be next to each other.

WHITE KING •
The range of the king is one square only, in any line direction.

• **EIGHT SQUARES**
The king can move to any of these eight squares, unless the square is attacked by a foe.

BLOCKED KING

In the position right, there are seven squares available to the king. It cannot move onto the square occupied by its own rook. Note that the king guards the rook and can recapture if the rook is taken by an enemy. However, if that enemy is defended by an ally, the king would not be able to recapture, as it would move into **check**.

WHITE KING •
This time the white king has one less square to choose from, leaving only seven possible.

• **ROOK ALLY**
Although the rook impedes the king, its own movement is not hampered by the king.

KING CAPTURE

This time the rook is an enemy **piece**, and the king can take it. If it does not, there are only three other squares available, as the rook is covering four squares in the king's field, and standing on the fifth.

RED SQUARE
The rook does not guard the square on which it stands, so is vulnerable to the king.

• **WHITE KING**
The king takes the rook, as it was not defended by one of its own team.

The rook

QUIZ BOX

Where can the white king move, and what can it capture?

The black knight is guarded by its king and bishop. The empty white squares either side of the knight are covered by the black king. The three squares to the white king's left are guarded by the bishop and the knight. White can move one square towards Black's side of the board, or capture the bishop.

CASTLING

Castling is the second special characteristic of the king

KING'S SIDE

Castling is the only time when two men are moved at once. The king and the rook are involved, recalling the rook's unofficial name. Neither piece must yet have been moved.

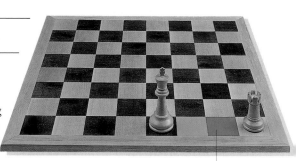

VACANT SQUARES •
The two squares between the king and the rook on the **king's side**, must be vacant. The king moves two squares towards the rook.

• **ROOK**
The rook is then moved to pass the king, to the square the king has just crossed.

SIMULTANEOUS MOVE
To carry out **castling** correctly, the king should theoretically be moved first, or both men moved at the same time.

• **ROOK**
The rook completes the move, on the square next to the king.

EXTRA CONDITIONS

Castling is not allowed if the king is already in **check**. The king is not allowed to move into check, so it may not castle onto, or across, a square that is attacked. It does not matter if the king has been in check earlier in the game, just as long as it did not move at the time, and is no longer in check, or required to move into check. Castling is not affected by the rook being attacked, or if it should cross a square that is threatened. In competitive play if you touch the rook first, your opponent can insist that you move only the rook.

DIFFERENT SIDES

Castling on the **queen's side** is less common for a number of reasons: firstly, three **pieces** – queen, bishop, and knight – must clear the **back rank** instead of just two – bishop and knight. Following **king's side** castling, the king guards the three pawns in front, if they are still in place, making a solid defense. On the queen's side, one of those pawns must have moved to release the bishop (except in freak cases where the bishop has been captured on its own square). With such a pawn move, the king may be exposed to **check** on the **diagonal** after queen's side castling.

THREE SQUARES •
These three squares must be empty for **queen's side castling**.

• **TWO SQUARES**
Black's king and rook have two vacant squares for **king's side castling**.

QUEEN'S SIDE

These boards show **queen's side castling**. The mechanics of the move are similar to **king's side** castling, but the two **pieces'** final position is nearer to the center of the **rank** on the queen's side.

• **TWO SQUARES**
The king moves along the **rank** two squares towards the rook.

• **ROOK'S SQUARE**
The rook moves right three squares, to the one the king has just crossed.

UNDEFENDED PAWNS

Note that after **queen's side castling**, the rook's pawn is no longer defended, either by the king or the rook. On **king's side** castling, the king guards the three pawns on the next **rank**, helping to make a strong defense.

ROOK'S PAWN SQUARE •
An unguarded pawn on this square is a weak link in the defense.

SKILL

4

THE PAWN

Definition: *The various moves of a pawn*

DAY 1

THE PAWN IS often considered as lowly. Many beginners find pawns little more than a nuisance, impeding the movement of the mighty **pieces**. With experience comes the discovery that the pawns shape the whole pattern of the game.

OBJECTIVE: To learn all the pawn moves and captures. *Rating* ••••

DIRECTION OF MOVE

Skilful handling of the pawns is a mark of a master. The pawn moves directly forward, one square at a time. It can never move backwards. A few centuries ago, the early phase of the game was speeded up by allowing any pawn, on its first move only, the option of advancing two squares. After that, the pawn can only move forward one square at a time.

SIMPLY TURNED
The pawn is usually the smallest and least ornate of all the chessmen. It has always been given the simplest treatment by the woodturner or sculptor. Pawns much like those in use today are to be found in illustrations of chess sets made as much as 750 years ago.

TWO SQUARES •
On its first move only, the pawn is allowed to move two squares forward if the player chooses.

• **ONE SQUARE**
For the first move if desired, and each subsequent move, the pawn moves one square forward at a time.

PAWN ATTACK

Unlike any other chessman, the pawn's capture differs from its move. It captures one square **diagonally** forward. It cannot capture two squares away on its first move, nor can it capture directly ahead. This difference in move and attack means it is the only man that can be blocked by an unprotected enemy.

• WHITE PAWN
White to move here has the choice of moving one square forward, or taking the rook.

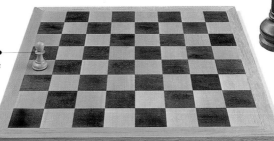

ROOK'S SQUARE •
As the pawn takes the opponent's square, it moves onto the adjacent **file**, and can advance only there.

The rook

QUIZ BOX

What pawn moves can be made by:
a) White, b) Black?

White, to move, has a choice of three possibilities; Black, to move, has four. The white and black pawns on the left block each *other. Neither can move. The white pawn on the right has a choice of moving straight forward, or of capturing either pawn on adjacent **files**. If it is Black's move, then either of the pawns on the right could move one square directly forward, or one of them could capture the white pawn.*

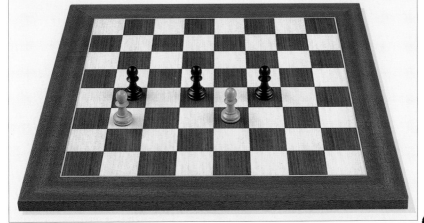

EN PASSANT

A rule to avoid bypassing pawn capture

DOUBLE MOVE

The two-square initial move of the pawn led to positions in which a player could use this extra leap to bypass an enemy pawn that could capture it, were it only allowed to move one square. To remedy this situation, the **en passant** rule was introduced.

ENEMY PAWN •
The enemy pawn has to have advanced three squares already.

• WHITE PAWN
White's pawn is about to make its first move.

THE FIFTH RANK
Only a pawn standing on a player's fifth **rank**, above for Black, can capture **en passant**. Beginners often have difficulty with this capture, but if the reason for its introduction is remembered the move follows naturally.

RIGHTFUL CAPTURE

By the **en passant** rule, the threatening pawn can capture the double-stepping enemy pawn as if it had moved only one square. The capturing pawn goes to the square the enemy pawn has crossed, and would be on had it only been allowed a single move, not the square that the enemy pawn newly occupies. The pawn is removed from the board, as with other captures.

THREATENING PAWN •
The black pawn threatens the square that the white pawn has bypassed.

• DOUBLE-STEPPING PAWN
White has moved two squares to avoid capture by Black's pawn.

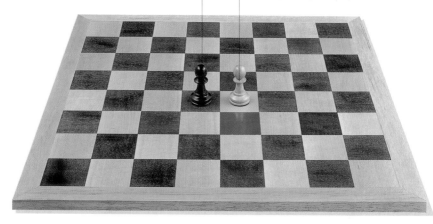

ACT FAST

En passant capture must be made immediately after the enemy pawn makes its big move, and no later. You might think that a **piece** could capture a pawn en passant. Illogically, this is not the case – it is a pawn's privilege.

• **MISSED SQUARE**
The black pawn has taken the square that the white pawn bypassed in its double move.

The white pawn is captured

QUIZ BOX

If White advances the pawn on the right by two squares can Black capture **en passant**? What about the pawn on the left?

If the white pawn on the left is removed from the board, the position shown is exactly that on

*the opposite page, so Black can capture **en passant** if the right-hand pawn advances two squares. Alternatively, if the left-hand pawn advances one square, Black cannot capture en passant because the white pawn used two separate moves to reach its destination.*

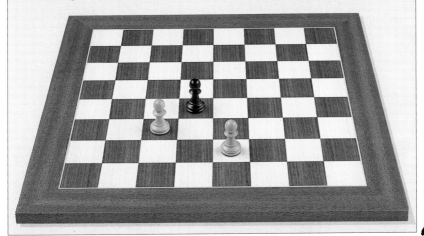

PROMOTION

When a pawn becomes a **piece**

SKILL
4

THE FINAL RANK

When a pawn reaches the far side of the board, as part of the same move it is removed from the board and a **piece** of the same color is substituted. This is known as **promotion**.

• **BLACK PAWN**
The pawn can advance one square and be **promoted**. In almost every case a queen is chosen, and so players often talk of **queening** a pawn.

• **WHITE KNIGHT**
The white knight can be captured by the new black queen, but it cannot threaten her.

QUEEN BY CAPTURE

In this **promotion**, the pawn has captured the knight to reach the edge of the board. It is theoretically possible for a player to have nine queens, but even having three is extremely rare.

PAWN QUEENED
Promotion is not conditional on the way a pawn reaches the furthest rank, or whether there is already a queen on the board.

UNDERPROMOTION

Underpromotion is when a **piece** of less value than the queen is chosen. There are occasions when it is more profitable to **promote** to a knight. A knight can give **check** from a square that no other piece can, so it is the most common choice other than a queen. Some computers for beginners do not offer underpromotion.

A pawn may become a rook, knight, bishop, or a queen

KNIGHT TO CHECK
Below: If White's forward pawn takes the bishop and becomes a knight, giving **check**, then it wins Black's queen. However, if the pawn takes the bishop and becomes a queen, Black takes the pawn in front of White's king and calls **checkmate** (see pp.44-45). Alternatively, if the white pawn advances one square and **queens**, Black's queen captures it.

• **KING**
The black king moves out of **check**, and the queen is lost.

• **BISHOP'S POSITION**
A white knight on this square **checks** the black king, and can take the black queen.

TWO OR MORE QUEENS

If a queen is not available because it is still in play, an inverted rook is often used, as it is the only **piece** that is stable when upside down. An alternative is to mark the pawn in some way, such as with a piece of string. In an emergency, anything will do – even a salt shaker. In practice, there is frequently a flurry of **exchanges** directly after **promotion**, so the long-term need for improvisation is actually extremely rare.

Inverted rook

Marked pawn

SKILL

5

CHECK

DAY 1

Definition: *An attacked king is said to be in* **check**

A THREATENED KING IS IN CHECK. If your king is attacked you must immediately relieve the check, on your next move. Similarly, if you give check your opponent must get out of it at once. At one time it was compulsory to say "check", but this is no longer the case. Strong players are expected to be aware of it, but among beginners it is a good idea to announce "check". Remember that one king cannot check the other, and players are not allowed to put themselves in check.

OBJECTIVE: To learn how to recognize **check**. *Rating* •••

THREATENED KING

The white king is in **check** and has a choice of two unattacked squares. If it moves into the corner, Black has two moves, either of which gives check. Both of these moves leave White with no move.

CORNER SQUARE •
With the white king in this corner square, the black queen can either move one square forward, or one **diagonally** right. Both these moves give **check**, with no legal reply for the king.

TAKE ONE STEP TO THE LEFT
The king's best move is to the square on its left, where it has greater freedom. The king can still be **checked**, but can escape.

• **WHITE KING**
When the king moves to this square, it cannot be trapped and the position is absolutely level.

ESCAPING CHECK

There are up to three ways to get out of **check**. The king can move, the attacking **piece** can be taken, or a man may be interposed between the attacking piece and the king. This last possibility cannot arise if the checking man is a knight or a pawn, due to their methods of capture. It is unusual for all three possibilities to be available in any given situation.

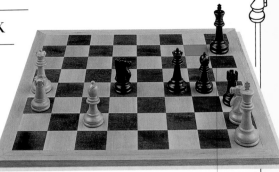

THREE OPTIONS
Black is in **check** from White's bishop, and all three ways of escaping check are available.

MOVE KING •
The best choice here is to move the king to the green square.

INTERPOSING A MAN
There are five ways here that a **piece** can be interposed. They all lose **material**. If the rook blocks the **check**, White takes it for nothing. If the queen blocks – on either of two squares – White wins the queen for the bishop by capturing it with check. If the knight blocks, White wins the queen in the same way as if the knight had captured the bishop. Finally, the bishop could be interposed, right.

BISHOP •
The black bishop has blocked the **checking** path of the white bishop, and no longer defends the rook.

• BLACK KING
The black king is shielded from attack on the **diagonal** by the black bishop.

WHITE ROOK •
White can take Black's rook with **check**. Black cannot recapture with the bishop.

CAPTURE •
The white bishop could capture the interposed **piece**, and give **check**.

TAKE THE CHECKING PIECE
The **checking piece** could be taken by the knight. However, this allows the white rook to take Black's rook, with check, and then win the queen on the following move.

WHITE QUEEN •
If the queen captures the knight to give **check**, it wins nothing. If the white queen takes the black queen, White wins, but not as quickly as when the rook is taken first.

CHECKMATE

*If the king cannot get out of **check** it is **checkmated***

WINNING THE GAME

Checkmate, or **mate**, ends the game. The player giving **check** has won. It is the only way to win, but most games end when a player **resigns**, rather than go through the dying agonies. As a rule though, beginners should not resign too hastily, for miracles may happen.

• WHITE QUEEN
The queen is not able to take the black rook to save the king.

WHITE KING •
The white king is in **check** by the black rook and all the means of escape are blocked.

WHITE IS MATED
In all these games White's king is **checkmated**. The **checking piece** cannot be captured, the check cannot be blocked, nor can the king move out of check.

• WHITE KING
When a king's own men block all of its escapes from **check**, it is known as a "smothered" **mate**.

BLACK KNIGHT •
The black knight's path cannot be blocked.

• WHITE ROOK
Without the rook, White could not lose, and might even win!

ROOK CHECK
As in the first example, top, no man can be interposed between the king and the rook, and neither can the rook be captured.

WHITE KING
The white king's escape is again blocked by its own men, so it is **mated**.

DISCOVERED CHECK

Check is sometimes given when a man moves from between a line piece and the enemy king. This is called discovered check, and is often lethal because the man that moves can attack another target. Here, the white bishop moves two squares towards the top left corner, attacking the queen and at the same time giving check by the rook. This wins the queen.

• **BISHOP'S MOVE**
The white bishop moves here, and the black king is exposed to **check** by the rook.

THE ALTERNATIVE DRAWS
Instead the bishop could have moved to the square on which White's queen began the game, again attacking the queen with the bishop and giving **check** at the same time. This time the black queen retreats to the square in front of the king, and the game is eventually drawn.

QUIZ BOX

With Black to move, how many discovered **checks** are there? Which is the strongest?

HINTS ON DOUBLE CHECK
A special form of discovered **check** can arise when the man moving also gives check. This is known as double check, and can be met only by a move of the king. It is not possible to capture two **pieces** at once, or to interpose on two different lines at the same time. In this particular example, a double check is not possible because the white king is on a dark-colored square, and this bishop only moves on light ones.

THE BEST MOVE
In this example, one square of the bishop's potential range is blocked by the black king, so there are eight discovered **checks**. *Only one gives* **checkmate** *at once. Three can give* **mate** *in two moves, one leads to mate in three moves, and three lead to no great advantage.*

If the bishop moves • to this square, White is **mated** *on the first move.*

SKILL

6

DRAW

Definition: *A game that is not won is a draw*

NOT ALL GAMES end in victory. The other outcome is a draw. The two players can agree between themselves to call the game a draw – maybe there is not enough **material** on the board. If a player has only a king, their opponent cannot **checkmate** with just a king, or a king and a knight, or a king and a bishop – try this out. There are three situations where a draw is laid down by the rules. Two are analyzed here; you are unlikely to meet the third.

OBJECTIVE: To learn the rules governing draws. *Rating* •••

STALEMATE

The first kind of draw occurs when the player to move is not in **check**, but has no legal move available. This is called **stalemate**, and frequently happens between beginners when one side has a queen and king and the other just the king.

WHITE IS STALEMATED
White, to move, is **stalemated**. It is against the rules to move your own king into **check**, and all three squares to which the white king might otherwise move are threatened by the black queen. Although the king is not in check at present, the game is over.

LUCK OR JUDGMENT?
Such endings can be accidental between beginners, but good players sometimes find such resources when desperate.

WHITE KING •
The white king is not allowed to move into **check** on any of the three attacked squares.

DRAW BY REPETITION

The second draw is when the same position appears on the board three times with the same player to move. If one player keeps **checking** the other with no escape, and no **mate** either, this is known as **perpetual check**.

PERPETUAL CHECK
In this desperate situation, White to play draws. White's queen goes straight forward to the enemy's first **rank**, giving **check**. Black has only one possible reply.

WHITE QUEEN •
As the white queen **checks**, the black king moves one square left, **diagonally**.

REPETITIVE MOVES
White's queen moves back on the shorter **diagonal**, giving check. Again Black has only one move. After these two moves have been played twice, the game is drawn by repetition of position, with **perpetual check**.

• ONE MOVE
Black has only one reply to each move.

• DIAGONAL PATH
The white queen goes backwards and forwards on this **diagonal**.

THE THIRD DRAW
The final kind of draw covered by the laws of chess arises if no pawn has been moved, and no capture has taken place for fifty moves, when a draw may be – but does not have to be – claimed.

NOW YOU CAN PLAY

You now know enough to play a legal game of chess. You have been given all the essential information, and nothing extra. Try out a few games with a friend or a computer, but don't expect to win. Be pleased if you play a whole game without moving a **piece** wrongly. A computer will tell you if you do so, a beginner might not. Two novices may be playing unaware that both kings are in **check**.

SKILL

7 SCORES

DAY 1

Definition: *Reading printed chess games*

YOU ARE CERTAIN to have the urge to win more often, and meeting
that need is the goal of the rest of the weekend. A vital aid to your
improvement is the ability to study instructive games. Chess
positions are usually shown in **diagrams**. The moves of the game
are written in a standard **notation**, so that any player can read them.
If you are to write down your games, read those in newspapers and
books, and generally progress, you must be familiar with its form.

OBJECTIVE: To learn how to use chess literature. *Rating* •••

DIAGRAM & MEN

On **diagrams**, the figurines are stylized
representations of Staunton men,
right, some of them just showing the
upper portion. Diagrams always
show Black playing from the top,
and White playing from the bottom.

The rook, R

The knight, N

The bishop, B

The queen, Q

The king, K

The pawn

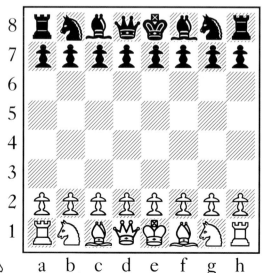

IDENTIFYING THE MEN
The **pieces** are identified by
their initial letter. As the king
and knight have the same initial,
"N" is commonly used for the
latter, although "Kt" is seen
occasionally. The pawn is not
often given its "P". On the
movement of a pawn, only
the arrival square is given.

COORDINATES
Numbers and letters are at the
sides of this **diagram**, which shows
the men in their initial **array**.
Your computer has these marks,
as might your ordinary board.
Each **rank** is numbered, 1 to 8,
starting on White's side. Each **file**
has a small letter, a to h, from the
queen's side to the **king's**.

THE SCORE

This **diagram** shows how the coordinates are used like map references, to give each square a unique identity. The moves are numbered from 1 onwards, in pairs of white and black moves. The **score** gives the initial, in capital letters, of the **piece** moved, and the square, in small letters, to which it moves. If two pieces of the same kind could move to one arrival square then part of the departure square's label is also given. Some **notation** uses the departure square every move.

	a	b	c	d	e	f	g	h	
8	a8	b8	c8	d8	e8	f8	g8	h8	8
7	a7	b7	c7	d7	e7	f7	g7	h7	7
6	a6	b6	c6	d6	e6	f6	g6	h6	6
5	a5	b5	c5	d5	e5	f5	g5	h5	5
4	a4	b4	c4	d4	e4	f4	g4	h4	4
3	a3	b3	c3	d3	e3	f3	g3	h3	3
2	a2	b2	c2	d2	e2	f2	g2	h2	2
1	a1	b1	c1	d1	e1	f1	g1	h1	1
	a	b	c	d	e	f	g	h	

1 e4 e5

On the first move of a game, White moved a pawn from e2 to e4, a double move, and Black replied by moving a pawn from e7 to e5.

7...Nxf2 8 Kxf2 dxe3+

Black's reply to White's seventh move is to move the knight, making a capture on f2. White's king recaptures on the same square; Black's d-pawn captures diagonally on the e-file giving check.

UNDERSTANDING THE SCORE

Left: The symbol x, before the arrival square, indicates a capture. On a pawn capture, the initial of the **file** of origin is given before the "x". Three dots in between the number and the move denote Black's move. The symbol +, indicates **check**. A pawn's **promotion** is shown by =, followed by the initial of its new **piece** status. **Castling** is shown by 0-0 on the **king's side**, and 0-0-0 on the **queen's side**.

CHECK THIS OUT

You can now read games in newspapers and books, but you will need practice. Try reading the moves below. Avoid positions that are described as **problems**, or have a caption such as "**mate** in 2" – they are not chess, but simply a close relation.

If Black takes the pawn in the middle with the bishop, this is shown as 1...Bxd4. White's move is usually described first, so the three dots show it is Black's move.

If White recaptures with the knight furthest from the king, this is 2 N5xd4. N5 indicates that it is the knight on the 5th **rank**, as they are both on the f-**file**.

Black now moves the rook furthest from the king onto the e-**file**, and this is shown as 2...Rhe8. Rh pinpoints the rook on the h-file. Both rooks are on the 8th **rank**.

8

PLAY

Definition: *Into battle, finding moves*

DAY 1

IN YOUR FIRST CHESS GAMES, you may struggle just to move the men correctly, and have little time for grand plans. Don't worry. It takes time before the moves will come naturally to you. When they do, you will want to know how to set about winning. It is important to realize that you cannot win unless your opponent makes a mistake – there is no possibility of creating a win solely out of your own genius.

OBJECTIVE: To learn how to form plans and find moves. *Rating* ••••

DEFENSE & ATTACK

In a well-played game, both sides try to create threats and to counteract those made against them. Eventually, one player cannot meet all the threats and concedes an advantage that the dominant player strives to increase.

EXPERT GAME

In this game between experienced players, play went 9 Na3 Qc7 10 Bd2 Nc6 11 Nb5 Qb8 12 Nd6+ Bxd6 13 exd6 d4 14 c5 a6 15 h4 h5 16 Bd3 b6 17 Bxg6 fxg6 18 Qxg6+ Kf8 19 Ng5 Nd8 20 Nh7+ Kg8 21 Nf6+ Kf8 22 Qe8 **mate**.

WHITE'S GRIP HERE •
Black's 13th move of a pawn to d4 is a blunder, allowing White to support the pawn on d6 with a pawn on c5.

• PAWN STRONGHOLD
The game has revolved around White's attempt to maintain the pawn on e5, and so the white queen is slightly out of play.

CHIGORIN–TARRASCH

Tarrasch took seven pages of a book for experienced players to explain this keenly-fought game between these two great players. The main strategies of the two sides are easy for a novice to follow, even if the tactics are still too complicated.

TO REACH THIS POSITION •
Play 1 e4 e6 2 Qe2 c5 3 g3 Nc6 4 Nf3 Be7 5 Bg2 d5 6 d3 Nf6 7 0-0 0-0 8 Nc3 a6 9 Bg5 h6 10 Bf4 b5 11 Rfe1 d4 12 Nd1 Nd7 13 Kh1 Re8 14 Rg1 e5 15 Bd2 Nf8 16 Ne1 Ne6 17 f4 Bb7 18 f5 Ng5 19 Nf2 Rc8 20 Qh5 Nh7 21 Nf3.

ATTACKS ON OPPOSITE WINGS
Above: White is committed to an attack on the **king's side**, and Black exerts pressure on the **queen's side**. 21...c4 22 Bf1 cxd3 23 cxd3 Ng5 24 Bxg5 Bxg5 25 Ng4 Kf8 26 Be2 Bf6 27 h4 Qd6 28 Nfh2 Ne7 29 Raf1 Ng8 30 Bd1 Rc7 31 Bb3 Rec8 32 Nf2 Bd8. Black needs to **exchange** off White's light-square bishop to control the c-**file**, so advances the pawn to a4, and maneuvers the bishop b7-c6-e8-f7-b3-d1 over six moves.

• TO REACH THIS POSITION
Play continues: 33 Qe2 a5 34 Nf3 a4 35 Bd1 Bc6 36 g4 f6 37 Nh3 Be8 38 Qh2 Bf7 39 a3 Bb3 40 Nf2 Bxd1 41 Nxd1 Rc2 42 Qg3 b4 43 axb4 Qa6 44 Nf2 Rxb2 45 g5 hxg5 46 hxg5 Rcc2.

BLACK PLAYS FOR A WIN
Above: The situation at the 46th move shows each side's central ideas in action. The game ended: 47 Ng4 Qd6 48 gxf6 Bxf6 49 Qh3 a3 50 Nxf6 Qxf6 51 Rg6 a2 – few beginners would consider this move – 52 Rxf6+ gxf6 53 Rd1 Rb1 54 Qf1 Rcb2 55 Nd2 Rxd1 56 Qxd1 Rxd2 57 Qc1 and not 57 Qxd2 a1=Q+.

WHITE LOSS •
The game closes this way: 57...Rxd3 58 Kg2 Rc3 59 Qa1 Rc2+ 60 Kf3 d3 61 Qd1 Rb2 62 Qa4 d2 and White **resigns**.

"TOUCH AND MOVE"

When it is your turn to play, only touch a man to move it, unless you warn your opponent first that you are adjusting it on its square. By the laws of the game, a player can insist that a man touched must be moved – "touch and move". If it cannot be moved, the king must be moved. If neither is possible there is no penalty. If you blunder, never ask your opponent if you can undo the move, and try to avoid players who ask for this privilege.

SKILL

8 CRAMPED POSITION

Black is to move in this position. There are no major threats being made by White, and none that can be made immediately by Black. Black has a cramped position and would benefit by **exchanges**, which White should try to limit. Black wants to get the queen's bishop into play, but 1...b6 allows 2 e4, giving White too much freedom in the center. A better move is 1...Nd5. 2 Bxe7 Qxe7 3 0-0 Nxc3 4 Rxc3 e5 might follow, and Black's position is good.

• QUEEN'S BISHOP
Black must try to get this bishop into play without creating a weakness.

EXPOSED BISHOP •
After 1...Nd5 this bishop is attacked twice and defended only once.

QUIET POSITION

White is to move. Contrary to first appearances 1 Nf4, frustrating 1...f6, can be played because 1...cxd4 2 cxd4 Nxd4 3 Nxd4 Qxd4 4 Bxh7+ exposes the black queen to capture. This is known as a discovered attack.

• BLACK PAWN
Black's main threat is to play this pawn from f7 to f6, where it would help to break up White's strong pawn formation in the center.

WHITE BISHOP •
White's bishop on c1 is tied to the defence of the b2-pawn, and cannot move to e3 to protect the d-pawn.

• WHITE PAWN
White's d-pawn is attacked three times, and the two knights appear to be tied to its defense.

MID-GAME

White to move as the **opening** phase is coming to an end. The natural plans here are for White to attack on the **queen's side**, and Black on the **king's** where each, respectively, exercises the greater control. Typical continuations are: 1 b4 Nh5 2 c5 Nf4 3 Bxf4 exf4; 1 Ne1 Nd7 2 Nd3 (aimed at strategical squares b4, c5, e5, and f4); 1 Bd2 Nh5 2 g3 f5 3 exf5 Nxf5. Choose your route according to how you feel most comfortable.

ALTERNATIVE IDEA
1 Nd2 is an odd looking move. The idea, in due course, is to put the knight on c4 –
1...Nd7 2 b4 f5 3 f3 Nf6 4 c5 f4 5 Nc4.

OVERLOADED PAWN •
The e7-pawn is **overloaded**, but 1 Nxd6 does not win a pawn: Black replies 1...Qh7+ 2 Kg2 Rc1 with a clear advantage.

DIFFICULT POSITION

White to move in this difficult position. 1 Re2 Rc2, **exchanging** rooks, looks better than 1...Rc1 2 Rxe7 Bxe7 3 Nxd6+ (discovered **check**) Kg7 4 Qf7+ Kh8 5 Qe8+ Kg7 6 Qxe7+ which gives a strong attack. 1 Rf2 would strengthen the defense of the knight on f5 in anticipation of Black's playing Rc3.

INFERIOR MOVES

Don't worry if you do not win quickly when your opponent makes a bad move. Be happy that you have the better position. If you are White here, after 1 e4 e5 2 Nf3 f6 you perhaps know that Black has played badly and can expect a quick win after 3 Nxe5 fxe5 4 Qh5+ g6 5 Qxe5+ Qe7 6 Qxh8. If 3...Qe7 instead, then 4 Qh5+ g6 5 Nxg6 Qxe4+ 6 Be2 Qxg6 would be a mistake.

MOVE THE KNIGHT •
After 3 Nxe5 Qe7, try the simplest response: 4 Nf3 Qxe4+ 5 Be2, or 4...d5 5 d3 dxe4 6 dxe4, and White is better placed than Black.

SKILL

9 MATERIAL

DAY 2

Definition: *Putting a value on each man*

SCALES OF VALUES for the chessmen, evolved over the years, can be helpful in assessing the usefulness of possible **exchanges**. It is important to remember that any scale is only a rough, general guide. There are many situations that are exceptions to the rule, and so using such equations may be inappropriate. The values shown in this skill are probably the most widely used. Once you know the worth of each man, you can judge whether exchanges favor one player.

OBJECTIVE: To learn the relative worth of each man. *Rating* ••

PIECE VALUE

The **pieces** are given values based on the number of pawns that would make an equivalent. These values apply only when other factors do not override them. This does not mean that in any given situation you could substitute men of equivalent value and not affect the game. In general, if the **material** on both sides is of equivalent value and neither side has a positional advantage, the game is evenly balanced.

UNIT OF SCALE
The pawn is the man of least worth, and provides the "unit" of scale. Bear in mind the warning that these scales only apply if other factors do not take priority. A pawn that is about to be **promoted** is obviously worth much more than one on its initial square.

THE PIECES
It is not possible to give **mate** with just a king and a knight, or a king and a bishop. Mate can be given with just a rook, or a queen, with the king. Due to this distinction, the knight and the bishop are known as **minor pieces**, and the queen and the rook **major pieces**.

All the pieces except the king have a value

ALL THE PIECES
Each **piece**, apart from the king, is assigned a pawn value, to the nearest "whole" pawn.

MINOR PIECES

The knight and the bishop are both valued at about three pawns. These two are known as **minor pieces**. Better players value the bishop slightly more than a knight, and two bishops are clearly better than two knights, or just one of each. Beginners usually find that they are able to do more with a knight than with a bishop.

Three pawns

The knight and the bishop are of about the same strength

THE ROOK

A rook is valued at five pawns. When a rook is taken for a knight or bishop, it is known as "winning **the exchange**". As a **major piece**, a rook and a king can give **mate**. No single **piece** can give mate without the help of the attacking king.

Five pawns

A rook is worth more than a **minor piece**

THE QUEEN

The queen is worth nine pawns. It is worth slightly less than two rooks, and about the same as three **minor pieces**. However this is not the case with inexperienced players who have not mastered the art of using their **pieces** in a coordinated manner. For them a queen is worth perhaps eleven pawns.

Nine pawns

A queen is worth as much as three **minor pieces**

MISUSE OF VALUES

After 1...e3+ 2 Kg1 exd2 3 Re8 **mate**, Black wins a queen at the expense of the game. Instead Black can play 2...Qb6 with an even game. White cannot take the pawn after 1...e3+ because after 2 Rxe3 or 2 Qxe3 Black replies 2...Ng4+.

SKILL
9 THREATS

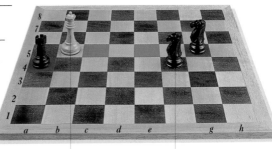

You are making a threat if you attack a man that is not being defended, or, even better, two undefended men at the same time. White attacks the black rook and also the knight on g5. Either can find a defence, but not both. If there was no knight on f4, Black's rook would be able to move to g4, taking itself out of danger, to a position guarding the knight on g5 at the same time.

• WHITE QUEEN
The white queen is threatening both the black rook and one of the knights simultaneously.

• BLACK KNIGHT
This knight blocks the rook's move to g4, where it would be safe and able to guard the other knight.

NO THREATS

You are not making a threat if you attack a defended man of lesser value. Left, White's queen is not threatening Black's rook, but the rook is threatening the queen. You will remember that the rook's value is five, while that of the queen is nine. An **exchange** would leave Black with only a **minor piece**, a bishop, and so the game would be a draw.

WHITE QUEEN •
The white queen is threatened by the black rook, which is of lesser value.

MULTIPLE ATTACK

During a game it often happens that something is attacked and defended many times, and you want to know if, after a series of captures and recaptures, you will win or lose **material**, or break even. Assess this game to see whether White can win a pawn on d4. The answer is no, since a **piece** is lost for the pawn when all the potential **exchanges** have been made.

BLACK PAWN •
Three white **pieces** – knight, bishop, and rook – and a white pawn threaten the black pawn on square d4.

• DEFENDED SQUARE
Four black **pieces** and a black pawn defend square d4, giving solid protection to black's pawn.

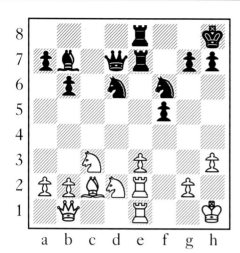

DEFENSE

Consider whether White will lose **material** by advancing the pawn on e3. It is easy to get muddled if you try to work this out move by move. The secret is to count how many times a man is attacked and how many defended. If attackers outnumber defenders, a capture can be made, otherwise not.

WHITE PAWN
If the pawn advances to e4, it is attacked and defended six times by each side, so it can be moved safely.

VALUES OF EXCHANGE
Before you rush ahead to capture you must also look at the values of the men involved. Here, they are equal, so the move can be made without loss. If, in the initial position, White's queen and bishop changed places, then White would lose the pawn.

*There would be an equal **exchange** of five **pieces**, and a pawn*

QUIZ BOX

CAN WHITE WIN A MAN?
In the situation, right, can White win a man, and would **material** be lost in doing so?

*White can get two pawns for a **piece**, but would be worse off. If White plays 1 Nxe4, then after 1...dxe4 2 Rxe4 Black has a value of 8 to White's 7, but this would not be enough to win. If rooks were then **exchanged** only White could win.*

WILL WHITE BENEFIT?
What will be the **material exchange** in this game, if White is to move first?

*White can get two **pieces** in **exchange** for the queen. White's value is 15, Black's 8. After the exchanges White has 5, Black has 0. With kings here, such an exchange would reduce White's lead, but give a cast-iron win.*

SKILL

10 OPENING

Definition: *Playing the first few moves*

DURING THE **OPENING** phase you aim to mobilize your pieces and control as much space as possible, particularly the center of the board, without losing time. The only **piece** that can move first is the knight, with a choice of two moves. After three moves by each player more than nine million different positions are possible, so it is better to understand the ideas behind the **openings**, rather than trying to memorize strings of moves.

OBJECTIVE: To learn the ideas behind the **opening** moves. *Rating* •••

POPULAR START

Look at the initial **array**, to count how many different first moves are possible. There are 20 possible first moves for White, and 20 for Black in reply. You will remember that the bishop and knight particularly (pp.24-25 and 30-31) have more power when they are near the center of the board, so an early task is to bring them out.

FIRST MOVE
Nothing much can be done until at least one pawn moves, and so the most popular first move for White is 1 e4. This attacks two squares in the enemy camp while unleashing the queen, and the king's bishop.

• **BLACK REPLY**
Black often replies 1...e5 to White for similar reasons.

SECOND STRING

The next most frequent **opening** move is 1 d4, with similar general aims. At first, you would do well to stick to one of these two openings.

BLACK RESPONSE
The tried and trusted reply 1...d5 is suggested here. 1...Nf6 is quite often played as an alternative.

WELL-KNOWN OPENINGS

These three positions show some famous, significant beginnings. On all these boards the characteristic move, unplayed, is indicated by green squares. In the Sicilian Defense, Black can reply differently to White's 1 e4, with 1...c5. On the board bottom left, White can offer a gambit, the King's Gambit (see also p.61). The first moves of perhaps the most popular **opening**, The Spanish Opening are bottom right. This is also known as Ruy López, after a 16th-century Spanish priest who wrote about it.

The Sicilian Defense

The King's Gambit

*The Spanish **Opening***

TARGET POSITIONS

Reaching a good position in spite of your opponent

IDEAL GOAL

This is an effective **opening** for White. No pawn has yet been moved unnecessarily, the **minor pieces** are on good squares, the king has **castled** away from the exposed center of the **rank**, and the rooks support each other.

OBSTACLE

Your opponent is the obstacle to your getting this position. You need to defend against enemy threats and to take advantage of errors.

BLACK QUEEN •
The queen on f6 removes the threat to the black bishop on c5.

SCOTCH GAME

This line demonstrates the main principles of **opening** play. Every move seeks control of the center, improves the mobility of the **pieces**, creates threats, or meets them. After 1 e4 e5 2 Nf3 Nc6 3 d4 exd4 4 Nxd4 Bc5 5 Be3 Qf6 6 c3 Nge7 the position is about equal. After 5 Be3 the threat by White is a discovered attack on the c5-bishop by 6 Nxc6, when Black must take the knight to save the queen.

DRAGON VARIATION

BLACK BISHOP •
The black bishop has moved onto the long **diagonal** to focus attack the center.

The Sicilian Defense (see **Openings** Box p.59), 1 e4 c5, is another way of exerting pressure on the center. The Dragon Variation goes 2 Nf3 d6 3 d4 cxd4 4 Nxd4 Nf6 5 Nc3 g6 6 Be3 Bg7. The bishop's development, attacking on the center along the long **diagonal**, is known as a *fianchetto*, an Italian term referring to the flank. After 7 Be2 Nc6 the position is about level. This situation can also arise in other ways.

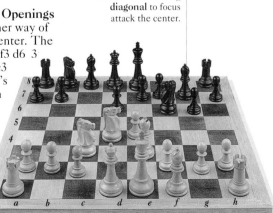

GRÜNFELD DEFENCE

In this different approach, White tries to control the center by direct methods while Black exerts pressure from afar. 1 d4 Nf6 2 c4 g6 3 Nc3 d5, the Grünfeld Defence. 4 cxd5 Nxd5 5 e4 Nxc3 6 bxc3 c5. Black will play Bg7, and in fact often plays it on the 6th move. An intensive battle for control of the center will follow.

PAWN CONTROL
Winning the pawn by 7 dxc5 is not a good plan. White will lose control of central squares and will be left with weakness on the c-**file**. Furthermore, Black regains the pawn easily.

• BLACK BISHOP
From g7 the black bishop will aim at the vital squares e5 and d4, as well as the weak pawn on c3 and the rook on a1.

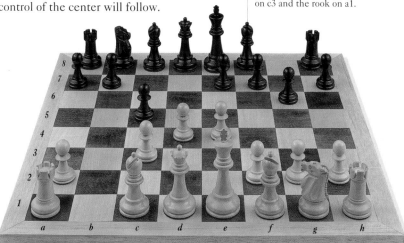

KING'S GAMBIT

This old-fashioned line has a high tactical content, making it excellent for instructional purposes. 1 e4 e5 2 f4, Black accepts the King's Gambit with 2...exf4 and now 3 Bc4 Qh4+ seems natural for Black, but it is short-sighted. It forces White's king to move because 4 g3 fxg3 5 hxg3 loses the rook. Play continues 4 Kf1 g5 to defend the pawn on f4, 5 Nc3 Bg7 6 d4 Ne7. Despite having lost the right to **castle**, White has more than compensation for the gambit pawn. Black's queen is ineffectively placed, and can be easily attacked.

BLACK QUEEN •
The queen is now in a vulnerable position.

• CENTRAL CONTROL
White has good control of the central squares of the board, despite the loss of a pawn.

SKILL

11

TACTICS

Definition: *The hand-to-hand combat of chess*

TACTICS IS THE ART of setting or answering short-term threats. Be alert to your chances without forgetting that your opponent is also making plans. Tactical skill decides almost all games of chess, and it can be developed only by practice. There are a few general tactical themes that crop up repeatedly in a variety of forms. These are **double attack**, **pin**, **overloading**, and **sacrifice**. In this skill, you will learn what each of these terms means. You will begin to recognize them in various shapes, and develop the skills to anticipate them.

OBJECTIVE: To be alert to giving and meeting threats. *Rating* •••

THE FORK

One **double attack**, partly considered in Skill 5 (pp.44-45), is discovered **check**, when the king and another target might be attacked at once. Another common double attack is called a **fork**, sometimes made by a pawn, but usually by a knight. If a knight forks a king and queen it is called a "family check".

• PAWN FORK
This is the second common type of **fork**, the pawn fork. The pawn is safe from capture.

• KNIGHT FORK
The knight attacks the queen and the rook. The queen can move to defend the rook.

A THIRD FORK
There is also another type of **fork**. This occurs when two men on the same **rank** or **file** might be attacked by a rook coming between them. A similar situation can arise with two men on a **diagonal**, by a bishop moving between them. Likewise, a queen could interpose in either case.

THE SKEWER

A **skewer** is a type of **double attack** by a line **piece**. An attacked man has to move to safety, exposing a second man further along the same line. The most lethal skewers are when the front man is a king that has to move out of **check**, or if a lesser **piece** threatens a queen.

WHITE BISHOP •
The bishop attacks the undefended knight, and the rook beyond.

UNDEFENDED KNIGHT
White's bishop threatens the undefended black knight. If it moves, the valuable rook will be taken in **exchange** for the bishop. Black's alternative is to lose the knight for nothing.

PREVENTING PROMOTION
White plays the rook to square h8. The only way that Black can prevent White's a-pawn from **queening** is to take it, replying 1...Rxa7. White now employs a **skewer** to win the rook, moving 2 Rh7+. This stratagem is often found in rook and pawn **endings**. After 1 Rh8, Black gets nowhere by playing 1...Kg7, attacking the rook because after 2 a8=Q the rook is now defended. Nor is 1...Ra3+ any use as the white king just moves to c4.

• **WHITE ROOK**
The white rook moves to free the pawn's advance.

QUIZ BOX

White can effect a **fork** or a **skewer** here. How?

The fork is achieved by 1 Bb5. A rook is worth 5 compared to the bishop's 3, so White must gain by an exchange such as 1...Raa6 2 Bxa6 Rxa6 or 1...Rcc4 2 Bxc4 Rxc4. In either case, White can follow with 3 Qf1+ winning the other rook as well. The skewer is 1 Qh4+ and, after the black king moves, 2 Qxa4.

SKILL
11 THE PIN

A common tactic, featured several times in most games, is the **pin**. A man is attacked along a line, and cannot move because a more valuable **piece** would be exposed along the same line. If the man is pinned to a king, it cannot move from the line, and has no defensive powers elsewhere. However, it can still give **check**.

PINNED KNIGHT
Above: Black's knight is **pinned** to the king. Other attackers can be brought in to increase the threat on the immobilized man.

BLACK KNIGHT •
The black knight is attacked twice, but only defended once, and so it must be lost.

PINNED BISHOP
Left: Black's bishop is **pinned**, attacked twice and defended once, but it can capture White's bishop. Black, to move, does not lose a **piece** this time.

• BLACK BISHOP
When both **pinner** and pinned are **pieces** of the same kind, the defender can capture the foe.

QUEEN PIN

If the shielded **piece** is anything other than a king, like a queen, the **pinned** man can move, but a player who tries to move it without making a plan first is foolish. The position, right, can arise in a well-known **opening**, the Queen's Gambit; this is after the fifth move.

• TO REACH THIS POSITION
After 1 d4 d5 2 c4 e6 3 Nc3 Nf6 4 Bg5, Black's knight is **pinned** to the queen, and 4...Nbd7 5 cxd5 exd5.

• DEFENSELESS PAWN
The **pin** appears to make the black pawn on d5 defenseless, as 6 Nxd5 Nxd5 7 Bxd8 wins the queen.

PLANNING AHEAD
After an apparently major loss, Black's reply bites back – 7...Bb4+, giving **check**. The only possible move for White is 8 Qd2. After 8...Bxd2+ 9 Kxd2 Kxd8 and Black finishes **the exchanges** with an extra **piece** in return for a pawn. Look twice if you see easy pickings.

OVERLOADING

When a man has too many defensive tasks it can be **overloaded**. One man could be guarding two others, and both are attacked by different enemy men. If one is captured, on recapture the other may no longer be defended.

OVERLOADED BLACK ROOK

Black's rook has too many tasks. It is guarding the knight and the bishop. After 1 Bxb5+ Rxb5 the bishop is unprotected. White can win the knight on b5 by a different method, as it is **pinned** to the king, – by 1 Rg5 – not 1 Nd4 (or c3) Bxd4 (c3).

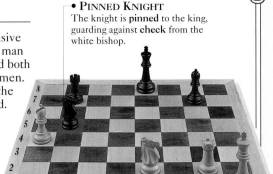

• PINNED KNIGHT
The knight is **pinned** to the king, guarding against **check** from the white bishop.

BLACK ROOK •
The rook only seems to guard the bishop on c5, but it is **overloaded**.

• BACK RANK
The **back rank** is also guarded by the black rook.

BACK-RANK MATE

Overloading is sometimes less obvious. Here, the black rook, defends a **piece** attacked only once, but it has another task. If White captures the bishop and Black recaptures, White's rook moves to the 8th **rank**, delivering **checkmate**. Play is 1 Nxc5 Rxc5 2 Rd8 mate. This kind of finish is known as a **back-rank mate**. Such a threat is common.

TWO PIECES ATTACKED

Right: White – played by Paul Morphy, a great figure in the chess world – moved 1 Qb4 from this position, attacking both queen and bishop. If 1...Qxb4 then 2 Re8+ Qf8 3 Rxf8 **mate**. A common device when two pieces are attacked is to move one so that it guards the other. Here 1...Qc8 fails because 2 Qxb7 Qxb7 3 Re8 mate.

ALTERNATIVE REPLY

An alternative plan is to move one **piece** with **check**, gaining time to move or guard the other one. Here 1...Qf4+ 2 Kb1 does not work because Black cannot both save the bishop and prevent **mate** from the white rook at the same time.

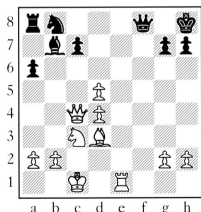

SKILL 11 — SACRIFICE

A successful **sacrifice**, where something is given up for nothing, or for a man of lesser value, is one of the great joys of chess. The intention when making the sacrifice is to finish better off. The typical sacrifice makes feasible what may seem impossible – a defensive **piece** could be knocked out, or a line opened for attack.

• UNGUARDED BLACK BISHOP
The bishop and rook are unprotected. On 1 Nd6 one of them would be lost but for the pawn on c7, and the unprotected rook on f6.

WHITE MOVE
If White begins by 1 Rxb6 cxb6 this allows 2 Nd6, right. If instead 1...Rxe4 then White replies 2 Rxb5, and not 2 fxe4 cxb6.

WHITE CHECK
With Black to move from the original position 1...Rxe4 would not win a **piece** (2 fxe4 Kxf6) because White would reply 2 Rxg6+.

ROYAL SACRIFICE

In this game, White has **sacrificed** two pawns to improve the **piece** development. White has an advantage in position, Black, in **material**. Positional advantages must be exploited or else they disappear. White is to move.

ROOK MATE
1 Qxd5+ exd5 2 Bb6+ is perhaps a harder move to find than the queen **sacrifice**, 2...axb6 is the only reply, 3 Re8 mate.

• QUEEN SACRIFICE
White can **sacrifice** the queen – admittedly too difficult for a beginner to find – 1 Qxd5+ exd5.

BETTER DEVELOPMENT
Above: White's **pieces** are all active, but neither of Black's rooks is doing anything useful.

OPTION 2
Did Black have options other than 1...exd5? If 1...Kc7 (or c8) 2 Bxa7+ rook **checks** Bc5 3 Rxc5 **mate**. If 1...Nd6 2 Qxg5.

THIRD MATE
Finally, if 1...Bd6 2 Qxb7 Qe7, this will prevent 3 Qd7 **mate**, 3 Qxa8+ Kc7 4 Qc6+ Kd8 5 Bxd6 and soon gives mate.

MATING SACRIFICE

A **sacrifice** can expose the enemy king so that it can be pursued to **mate**. White's attack is strong, but 1 Qxh6 is the surprise. 1...gxh6 and 2 gxf7+ is double **check**. If 2...Kf8 3 Rg8 mate, and if 2...Kh7 3 g8=N+, **underpromoting**, 3...Kh8 4 Rg8 mate.

GREEK GIFT

Here White opens Black's position with a **sacrifice** of a type that happens so often, it even has its own name – the Greek Gift. 1 Bxh7+ Kxh7 2 Rh3+ Kg8 3 Qh5. You will find that tactical skill wins more games than anything else.

WHITE BISHOP •
White **sacrifices** the bishop to open up Black's defense.

AVOIDING MATE
Black can prevent **mate** by 3...Bh4 4 Rxh4 Qxh4 5 Qxh4, reaching the position, right. 2...Bh4 3 Qh5+ Kg8 4 Rxh4 comes to the same end.

COMBINATION
A number of tactical elements woven together, to gain some particular advantage is known as a **combination**. A successful one is always a surprise, at least one element looking impossible at first glance.

A GAMBIT

Giving up a pawn early in the game to speed up development of **pieces**, is a gambit. After 1 e4 e5 2 Nf3 Nc6 3 d4 exd4, the Scotch Game. Here White plays a gambit, 4 c3 dxc3. White can reply 5 Nxc3, or extend the gambit by 5 Bc4, with a strong attack after 5...cxb2 6 Bxb2.

SKILL
12 STRATEGY

Definition: *Chess generalship*

THERE IS A QUIP that tactics is what you do when there is something to do, and strategy is what you do when there is nothing. Tactics is largely concerned with creating and responding to immediate threats. Strategy – improving one's position and weakening the opponent's – revolves around long-term plans.

OBJECTIVE: To be able to make long-range plans. *Rating* ••••

STRATEGIC AIMS

Even great players do not have one plan for the whole game. Strategic aims are modified throughout play in response to the other player's moves. You may feel that your opponent's **queen's side** pawns are weak and try to exploit this. Your rival might respond by creating a diversion on the **king's side**. You then have to consider whether you are able to complete your own plans first. You might wish to abandon your original strategy at this point altogether.

BATTLE OF HASTINGS

Below: White is to move in this position from a game played at Hastings in 1955. For strategical reasons, White wants the bishop to be on the h3-c8 **diagonal**.

WHITE BISHOP •
White moves the bishop tactically, 1 Bg4 Qc7 2 Bf5.

KNIGHT OUT •
This **piece** is ill placed, and has to be defended.

TERMINATOR
Play continued 2...Kf7 3 Rh7+ Ke8 4 Rah1 Qb7 5 Rh8 and Black **resigns**. The powerful bishop cuts off the black king's escape route.

• BISHOP
The importance of the bishop is evident in this alternative line: 2...Rh8 leads to 3 Rxh8 Rxh8 4 Rxa5 Qxa5 5 Qxe7+ Kg8 6 Be6 **mate**.

MATING STRATEGY

Had Black replied 1...Qxg4 in the game opposite, 2 Qxe7+ Rf7 – the best move – as 2...Kg8 or Kg6 is met by 3 Qh7 **mate**. Play continues 3 Rh7+ Kxh7, (as 3...Kg8 4 Qxf7 **mate**, or 3...Kg6 4 Qxf7+ Kf5 5 Qe6+ Kg6 6 Qxg4, with a decisive advantage in **material**). 4 Qxf7+ Kh8 or Kh6 5 Rh1+ and Black's queen has to be given up, 5...Qh4, to prevent immediate mate.

• **BLACK KNIGHT**
After 6 gxh4 Black has a hopeless knight and rook against a queen and rook.

DUD PAWNS
Black's pawns are on the wrong colored squares to block the bishop.

QUICK MATE

A third possible response for Black is 1...f5, then 2 Qxg5+ Kf7 3 Bh5 **mate**. All moves have a tactical element, and positional moves often carry simple threats. A simple mating threat might be met only at the cost of a pawn weakness. The aim is strategical, but the means tactical.

ARCH BISHOP •
Once occupying the square f5, the bishop dominates the **diagonals** h3-c8 and b1-h7.

POSITIONAL MOVE

A knight on an outer square can be better placed centrally, two moves away. If you can make one or both moves with threats you can save time.

STRONG WHITE
1 Nb5 threatens 2 Nc7+, **forking** king and rook. 1...Qd8, "undevelops" the queen. Then after 2 Qd3 Ke7 3 c4 White has a strong position.

• **KNIGHT MOVE**
Black loses a pawn to 1 Nb5 with 1...Ke7, as after 2 Qd3 Qf6 3 Nc7 Rb8, 4 Nd5+ **forks** the king and the queen. The aim of 1 Nb5 is to improve White's position, but the execution is tactical.

SKILL

12 DOUBLED ROOKS

Positional moves improve **piece** disposition, increasing their mobility while commanding as many squares as possible. For example, both rooks on the same **file** make a formidable force. This is **doubling** the **rooks**. Play, right, went 1 Rhd1 fxg5 2 Rd6+ Kf7 3 Bh5+ Ke7 4 Bxg5+ Kf8 5 Rf1+ and Black **resigned** rather than lose a piece.

DOUBLED ROOKS •
Black has **doubled** the **rooks** on the h-file. Even better is an **open file** – one with no pawns on it.

AVOIDING MATE

This game ended 1 Rg7+ Kh8 2 Nf8 and Black can avoid 3 Ng6 **mate** only by 2...Rxf8, when 3 Rh7+ Kg8 4 Rcg7 mate follows. Beginners do well to look for **checks** in desperate situations.

• DOUBLED ROOKS
White's rooks are **doubled** powerfully on the 7th **rank**. Had the black pawn on a3 been on a2, Black could have won the game.

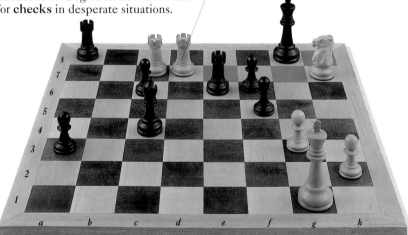

"SPITE CHECKS"
It is true that Black could have played 2...Re1+ 3 Kf2 Re2+ 4 Kf3 Bd5+ 5 Kxe2 Bc4+ 6 Kf2 before capturing the knight, but these **checks**, known as "spite checks", serve no purpose but to delay **mate**. Until you become skilful at visualizing positions, you are justified in making "spite checks". Sometimes you will find unexpected resources, such as **stalemate**.

• NO CHECKS
Black has run out of **checks** and can delay **mate** only by 6...Bf7 7 Rcxf7 Rxf8 8 Rh7+ Kg8 9 Rfg7 mate.

OUTPOSTS

When in the opponent's half of the board, a **piece** guarded by a pawn that is not open to attack from a pawn is an **outpost**. One great player said that if he could get a well-established piece like this knight on e6, the position was so strong, he could go to sleep for the rest of the game.

• WHITE KNIGHT
This knight, an **outpost**, was so strong that by the time it left its square 20 moves later, White's advantage was decisive. This game was between a World Champion, Lasker, and his successor, Capablanca.

BLACK RESIGNATION
Later in the game, Lasker played the white knight from e6 to c5, attacking both the black rook and the bishop. If the rook moves along the **file**, the bishop will be unguarded. If it moves along the **rank**, White plays 38 Nxb7 Rxb7 39 Nd6+ **forking** Black's king and rook with **check**. The game ended 37...Bc8 38 Nxd7 Bxd7 39 Rh7 Rf8 40 Ra1 Kd8 41 Ra8+ Bc8 42 Nc5 and Black **resigned**.

• FILE
White's position is strong with the rooks **doubled** on the open h-**file**. White controls most of the board, and has great mobility.

QUIZ BOX

If you are White, where lies your strength, and what should you play?

*Your strength lies in the command of the squares d5 and e4 and the associated weakness of Black's **backward pawn** on d6. Therefore you should apply pressure on the d-file by **doubling** your **rooks**, Rd3 followed by Rcd1. Now, as White you can win the pawn on d6 in half a dozen moves.*

SKILL

13 ENDGAME

Definition: *The phase when few men remain*

SOME OF THE MOST scientific teachers begin with the **endgame**, believing that this gives the opportunity to master the **pieces** one by one. However, most of us want to start playing as soon as we can. A few games later we feel the need to know more about the **ending**. Skill in the endgame is a mark of a master.

OBJECTIVE: To learn the basic principles of **endgame**. *Rating* ••••

PIECE ENDINGS

All of these basic **mates** *call for the attacker's king to be actively deployed*

QUEEN POSITIONS

Many beginners do not know how to give **mate** with just a queen and king against a king. Often they try without using the king and find that they have given **stalemate** instead. The defending king must be driven to the edge of the board in each case. Here are two typical mating positions with a queen, which should not take more than 10 moves from anywhere.

WHITE KING •
The white king is trapped, as there are no squares to which it can move without moving back into **check**.

MATING WITH A QUEEN
Left: If the queen were on d3 instead of a1 on this board, White to move is **stalemate**. If your queen does not give **check**, make sure the enemy king has a move.

• **WHITE KING**
Remember that a king cannot move to any square next to the opposing king.

ROOK POSITIONS

The rook and the queen are called **major pieces** because they are the only pieces that can force **mate** with the help of just a king. The rook **ending** is almost as simple as the queen's, and crops up regularly. To give mate, the attacking king must be actively utilized to prevent the defending king leaving the side of the board.

• **BLACK ROOK**
The rook gives **check** to the white king on this rank, from which the king cannot escape.

LEAST MOVES
Above: This **mate** can be forced in 16 or fewer moves from anywhere on the board.

WAITING MOVES
Left: Sometimes a move has to be "lost" to ensure the attacking king confines the defender to the side of the board. In this position, 1...Kb3 goes nowhere after White plays 2 Kc1. Instead, moving the rook to e2, g2, or h2, leads to **mate**, for example, 1...Rh2 2 Ka1 Kb3 3 Kb1 Rh1 mate. An alternative is 1...Rf1+ 2 Ka2 Rh1, which is another waiting move, answered by 3 Ka3, the only move, and 3...Ra1 mate.

• **WHITE KING**
The white king only has two possible moves in this position.

• **MOVE THE ROOK**
Moving the rook to h2 is more productive than closing in with the king.

QUIZ BOX

You are White and move first. How long does it take you to force mate? Try several times before you read on. Can you do as well? Can you do better?

1 Kb2 Ke5 2 Kc3 Ke4 3 Rh5 Ke3 4 Re5+ Kf4 5 Kd4 (Black's king is confined to 12 squares) 5...Kf3 6 Re4 (now 9 squares) 6...Kg3 7 Ke3 Kg2 8 Rg4+ Kh3 9 Kf3 (now 3 squares) 9...Kh2 10 Kf2 Kh3 11 Ra4 Kh2 12 Rh4 mate. Note White's waiting move, 11 Ra4. In fact any square on that rank, except h4, would serve as well. This example demonstrates a number of principles:

the defending king has to be driven to the edge of the board; the other king must be used as an attacking piece; the rook gradually draws a cordon; near the end, a waiting move is often needed to force the king into direct opposition.

13 TWO PIECES

Forcing a **mate** with just two bishops, or a bishop and a knight, is more difficult than with a **major piece**. Mate cannot be forced with two knights. In all cases with **minor pieces** the king has to be driven into a corner that can be covered by a bishop. Mate with two bishops is the easier of the two possibilities, taking a maximum of 19 moves.

• **WHITE KING**
The king must be on a corner square in order to **mate** with two bishops.

• **TWO BISHOPS**
Having two bishops means that the attacking side can use any of the four corners for **mating** purposes.

USING A KNIGHT
Even good players can struggle to **mate** with a knight and a bishop. Reaching the position, left, can take as many as 33 moves from an unfavorable start.

• **CORNER**
The king cannot be **mated** in a light corner, a8 or h1.

PAWN ENDINGS

*Pawn **endings** often arise. Just one pawn may be enough for victory if it can reach its **promotion** square*

PAWN QUADRANT

The area tinted blue represents the square of the pawn, or quadrant. A defending king that can enter the box can catch the pawn. As the pawn advances the box becomes smaller. If Black is to move, 1...Kf8 (or f7), the king will reach the **queening** square a8, in time to catch the pawn.

WHITE TO MOVE •
If it is White's move, then 1 a4, and the quadrant becomes 5 x 5 squares, instead of 6 x 6, and the Black king cannot enter.

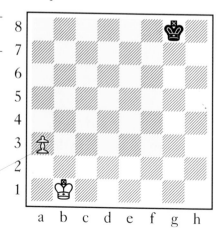

REARMOST PAWN •
This pawn is safe from capture. Black's king has to stay within the f-pawn's quadrant (f5-c5-c8-f8). White's king need not act quickly.

• FRONT PAWN
If Black plays 1...Kd6, White can reply 2 f6. Following moves would be 2...Ke6 3 e5.

TWO PAWNS

Until the white king has been brought into the fray, the pawns, here, cannot advance without being lost. However, they are safe where they are. If the black king takes the backward pawn, the forward pawn advances and Black is never able to get into the pawn quadrant to capture it.

DECISIVE POSITION
This and similar positions often arise. Make sure you know who will suffer from having to move first.

LONE PAWN

White to move in this position draws only. Knowledge of this will improve your result in many a game: Black to move loses. If you are White in this kind of **ending** you must reach this situation with Black to move. 1 Kc6 is **stalemate**; any other move loses the pawn. If it is Black's move, then 1...Kb7 is the only possibility, 2 Kd7 and the pawn is **promoted** on the next move, enabling White to have a clear win.

PAWN ADVANCE
Black to move and after 1...Kc7 2 Kc5 Kd7 3 Kb6 Kc8 4 Kc6 Kd8 5 Kb7, the pawn **queens**.

CRITICAL POSITION

This is the kind of critical position that often happens. Black to move will lose; White to move draws. 1 Kc5 Kc7 2 Kd5 Kd7 and Black continues to "take the opposition", that is, face the other king. The alternative is 1 c5 Kc7 2 c6 Kc8 with a draw, e.g. 3 Kb6 Kb8 4 c7+ Kc8 to a position like that above. Thirdly, 3 Kc5 Kc7 4 Kd5 Kc8, to continue as before.

SKILL

14 HANDLING PAWNS

Definition: *Moving pawns with a purpose*

LEARNERS TEND TO DESPISE pawns, believing that they rarely do anything exciting and just get in the way of the **pieces**. Accomplished players know better. The win of a pawn can be enough to lead to victory, so they should not be taken lightly. Significantly, it is the pawn formation, or skeleton as it is known, that shapes the character of the game. Unlike the pieces, the pawns can move forward only – there is no going back.

OBJECTIVE: To know the good, the bad, and the ugly structures. *Rating* •••••

PAWN FEATURES

Two pawns of the same color on one **file** are called **doubled pawns**. In itself this is generally regarded as a small weakness, but it may have compensations, such as making an adjacent file available for a rook, or strengthening an important square.

THE GAME
Left: This pawn skeleton (isolated below) can arise in the French Defense 1 e4 e6. The following moves are 2 d4 d5 3 Nc3 Bb4 4 e5 Ne7 5 a3 Bxc3+ 6 bxc3.

ISOLATED PAWN •
White has an **isolated pawn** on the a-file, so it can only be defended by **pieces**.

SECOND FILE •
White has the possibility of pressing on the b-**file**, with, for example, a rook on b1.

THE PAWN SKELETON
With this kind of skeleton, White is likely to attack on the **king's side** where a defending knight cannot use its natural square, f6.

• DOUBLED PAWNS
White has **doubled pawns** on the c-**file**. Neither of these can be defended by allied pawns.

DUAL NATURE

Early in the game, pawns should not be advanced without reason, and are mainly used defensively. At the end of the game, their value increases, they become more aggressive, and will head for **promotion** as rapidly as possible.

THE GAME
This is a position that can arise in the Caro-Kann Defense: 1 e4 c6. The moves could have been 2 c4 d5 3 exd5 cxd5 4 cxd5 Qxd5 5 Nc3 Qd6 6 d4 Nf6 7 Nf3 e6.

• **BLACK'S PAWNS**
Black's pawns are free from weakness, but they have less control of the center than White's d-pawn.

• **BLACK PAWN**
The pawn on e6 is prevented from advancing by the pawn on d4.

ISOLATED PAWN •
White has **isolated** queen's **pawn** on the d-**file**, which cannot be defended by another pawn.

ISOLATED QUEEN'S PAWN
An **isolated** queen's **pawn** is a feature so common that its abbreviation, IQP, is sometimes used when talking about it.

QUIZ BOX

Study the pawn formation here. You are White – how will you play? A clue: if Black's king moved, you could win the pawn on f6.

HINTS ON FORWARD MOTION
The pawn cannot go backwards. Moves are irretrievable, but weak players often move a pawn aimlessly if they can't think of anything useful to do with the **pieces**. Pawn moves that strengthen the position can usefully be played in such a situation. In the position here, it is the availability of spare moves that enables White to win.

ONE SOLUTION
The solution is to exhaust Black's pawn moves until a king move is forced: 1 g4 h6   2 h3 a6 3 a3 a5   4 a4 b6   5 b3. Now Black can choose which way to lose, 5...h5   6 gxh5, or 5...Ke8 6 Kxf6 Kf8   7 f5 Kg8   8 Ke7 Kg7   9 h4 Kg8 10 f6 Kh7   11 Kxf7 and White will soon be able to promote the f-pawn.

WHITE PAWNS •
Use the white pawns to exhaust Black's pawn moves.

SKILL

14 PASSED PAWN

A pawn with no enemy pawn ahead on its **file**, or adjacent ones, is a **passed pawn**. Only **pieces** can block its quest for **promotion**. It is usually regarded as beneficial, even when it is **isolated**.

WHITE PASSED PAWN •
White has two **passed pawns**, one on a5 and one on e5.

• BLACK PASSED PAWN
Black has a **passed pawn** on d5, and an **isolated pawn** on g7.

PASSED PAWN TO MATE
To get a **passed pawn** White **sacrifices** a piece, 1 Nxd6 Rxd6 2 Red3, **doubling** the **rooks**, 2...Rfd8 (2...Rxc6 3 Qxf8 **mate**) 3 Rxd6 Rxd6 4 Rxd6 cxd6 5 c7, the pawn advances, 5...Qe6 (to cover the **queening** square c8) 6 Qxd6 Qc8 (6...Qxd6 7 c8=Q+) 7 Qd8+ Qxd8 8 cxd8=Q mate.

BACKWARD PAWNS

A **backward pawn** is one on an otherwise **open file** that is held back by an enemy pawn on an adjacent **file**, and cannot use an allied pawn to defend it or help it to advance.

PAWN WEAKNESS
Usually a **backward pawn** is a weakness, especially if an enemy advances along its **file**, without fear of being driven off by a pawn.

• BACKWARD PAWN
Black has a **backward pawn** on e6. It cannot be defended for long: 1 Bh3 Qe8 2 Qe2 Qg6 3 Nxe6 Bxe6 4 Qxe6+ and White wins quickly.

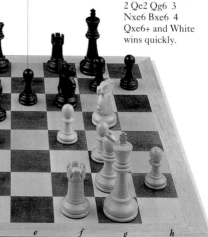

HOLE IN FORMATION

If in your half of the board, there is a square that can be invaded by a **piece** that cannot be driven off by a pawn, you have a **hole** in your formation. This gives your opponent an **outpost**. A **file** with no pawn of either color on it is an **open file**.

• BLACK HOLES
The squares d6 and g5 are **holes** in Black's pawn formation, and occupied as **outposts** by White.

• WHITE HOLES
White has a **hole** at e4, and another at g4, but they are less significant than Black's, because Black is not able to use them.

PINNED BISHOP •
Black's bishop on c6 cannot occupy the **outpost** on e4 because it is **pinned** to the rook by White's queen.

PAWN SKELETON
The pawns on the d-, e-, and f-**files** prevent Black's four **pieces** from working together. White's pieces are all in strong positions.

QUIZ BOX

Examine this position: it is from a World Championship, with Black to move. This position is extremely difficult to assess, but you will be able to catch some of the flavor and subtlety of grandmaster chess. The game revolves around the pawn formation. Most players would favor White's position, but few would find Black's move.

Black's 42...c5 appears to give White a strong passed pawn after 43 d5, but Black maneuvered his knights to e5 and d6, blocking the pawns and in due course made good use of his extra pawn on the queen's side. White

cannot play 43 dxc5 because the rook on d2 is unprotected. Although Black (Petrosian) won the game, experts believe that White (Botvinnik) might have been able to draw the game by sacrificing a central pawn.

SKILL

15 BEST MOVES

Definition: *Analyzing the current position*

DAY 2

IF FINDING THE BEST MOVE were easy, chess would have died out centuries ago. It is impossible to do every time and hard to achieve consistently. Those who are successful cannot explain it. Grandmasters do not consider more moves than weak players – the opposite is true. The better the player the fewer moves they examine.

OBJECTIVE: To learn a systematic approach to analysis. *Rating* •••

FINDING MOVES

If there are 30 possible moves, a top player would only give two or three profound study. Computers look at every possible first move, and weak players are nearly as unselective. There are occasions when there is only one way of getting out of **check**. These are **forced** moves. This term is also used when there seems to be only one sensible reply, but it pays to think twice before making the "forced" move.

FIVE WAYS TO MATE
Above: White's move, 1 Kh1 is **forced**. Black must now avoid careless moves, such as 1...Kf2 – **stalemate**. Instead, 1...Qg4 2 Kh2 (forced) Kf2 3 Kh1 (forced) and Black has a choice of five moves that give **mate**.

FORCED REPLY
White has just played 1 Qb5+. Black could play 1...Qc6 but would have two **isolated pawns** after 2 Qxc6+, and so prefers 1...Qxb5. White could play 2 Rfe1+, but is better kept as a threat, e.g. 2 Nxb5 Rc8 3 Rfe1+ Be7 4 Nd6+, to win a rook for a knight.

KNIGHT FORCE
White's reply is more or less **forced**, 2 Nxb5, although 2 Re1+ is possible first.

STRATAGEM

Sometimes a little stratagem can be introduced, which then changes the situation. In a World Championship match, Fischer-Spassky, Black played 1...Qxd2. After 2 Nxe7+ Kf8 3 Rxd2 Kxe7 4 Rxc4 winning Black's e-pawn.

MATERIAL •
Here the value of White's men totals 31 points to Black's 30.

REFLEX ACTION
When your queen is captured by the opposing queen, it is instinctive to want to recapture immediately. There may be a better move, however.

ISOLATED PAWN
Right: This is the position after the **combination**. White won a pawn and left Black with an **isolated** d-**pawn**. At that level, this gave a decisive advantage for White. Earlier, Black had **sacrificed** the **exchange** to win a pawn and pressure. Now both are lost.

MATERIAL •
Now the value of White's men is 18 points to Black's 16.

QUIZ BOX

White to move. What is the best way of meeting the threat to the queen? White found a move that made Black **resign** at once. Can you see it? When your queen is attacked, another reflex action, like the one above on the Stratagem board, is to consider nothing other than moving it. Sit on your hands for a moment and look around the board. Can you meet aggression with aggression?

After 1 Nd5, White threatens 2 Qxg7 mate. If Black prevents this by 1...Bxd4, then 2 Nxe7+ followed by 3 Bxd4 wins a piece. The lesson is that you should not look only at defensive moves when attacked. Had White been forced to move

*the queen, for example 1 Qe3, then Black could have won a pawn by 1...fxe4, because after 2 Qxe4 Qxe4 3 Nxe4, Bxb2 wins a piece. After 1 Nd5 Bxd4 2 Nxe7+ Black's king has to go to g7 or h8, and 3 Bxd4 gives **check**, allowing a pawn capture, 4 Nxc6.*

SKILL

15 SEQUENCE

Ask yourself two questions: what are the requirements of the position, and what first moves should you consider? If you are in the middle of a **combinational** sequence, don't make the move you previously analyzed without checking that it is still the best. In this position, White saw that he could win a **piece**. After 1 Ng3 Qxf4, he went on with 2 Nxe4 and won in 16 moves.

WHITE KNIGHT •
After 1 Ng3 Qxf4, White could have found 2 Nh5+, **forking** Black's king and queen to win instantly.

KING'S MOVE •
Black moves 1...Kf5, if you see the purpose you could play 2 Rc5+ with an easy win.

UNEXPECTED REPLY

Your opponent's last move may appear irrelevant to you, but try to understand their plans. You have White and expect to win easily after 1...Ra8 2 c7 Kd7 3 Kg6 Rc8 4 Kxg7. Black plays 1...Kf5, obviously a pointless move, making it easier for you to **queen** your pawn. Instead, 2 c7 Rh6+ 3 gxh6 (**forced**) g6 gives **mate**!

DISCOVERED ATTACK

DANGEROUS SQUARE •
The white knight is better not moving to g8, where the reply 1...Rxg8 will **pin** the white queen, preventing 2 Qxb2.

In a clearly tactical situation, look for moves that make or meet threats. White to move. Black's queen attacks the rook and the f6 knight. White cannot move one to defend the other, or cover them both with a third **piece**. As Black's queen is unguarded, White's knight can move with **check**, opening up the **diagonal** between the queens. White has two ways to do this, but they are not equally good. 1 Nd5+ is better, as after 1...exd5 2 Qxb2, White wins.

LINES OF PLAY

Before you analyze in depth, try to find quickly which first moves are worth examining. Glance at any **check** you or your rival might make, to see if it contains any hidden threats. Look in more detail at the candidate move that feels best. Judge the position a few moves further on. Now analyze the next best first move in a similar way, and so on. Even when you think you have made your choice, have a quick look at it again to see if your analysis still holds true.

ROOK THREAT •
Black threatens Rxd2, gaining for Black a small profit, two knights for a rook, after 2 R (or Q) xd2 Qxb3. 2 Nxd2 loses the rook on a2, 2...Qxa2.

• BISHOP THREAT
Black threatens Bd3, so a move by the queen or the rook on f1 looks a possible way of avoiding the loss of the **exchange.**

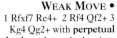

THE CANDIDATES

Perhaps 1 Nc1, 1 Rfa1, 1 Rd1, and 1 Qd1 are the candidate moves. However, 1 Nc1 still allows 1...Bd3 (2 Nxd3 Qxa2), and 1 Rd1 is suspect (see below). The other two appear to work. In the light of your deeper knowledge of the position, see if there are other candidates. With your fuller understanding of the situation, you might like to consider alternatives.

• POSSIBLE MOVE
1 Rfd1 looks doubtful after 1...Rxd2 2 Raxd2 Qxb3 3 Rd7, although the control of the d-**file** might be sufficient compensation.

MASTERFUL MOVE

If it is your move with the white men, make a list of your candidate moves. Your rook on f3 is attacked, and also Black has a strong threat of Re4+. You might pick 1 Rbxf7 and 1 Rfxf7, but they are not the best. If 1 Rbxf7 Re4+ 2 R3f4+ Qf2+ (the rook on f4 is **pinned**), 3 Kg5 Qg3+ 4 Rg4 Qe3+ 5 Rff4, and White should win. After 1 Qg7+, Black is defeated. **Mate** follows 1...Kxg7 2 Rfxf7+ Kg8 3 Rg7+ Kh8 4 Rh7+ Kg8 5 Rbg7 mate.

WEAK MOVE •
1 Rfxf7 Re4+ 2 Rf4 Qf2+ 3 Kg4 Qg2+ with **perpetual check,** and so only drawing.

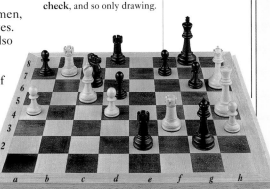

AFTER THE WEEKEND

Making giant strides

ONLY YOU CAN DECIDE how far you want to improve your play. If you simply want to enjoy social chess, you may find that occasional games with your friends are sufficient to consolidate the skills you have acquired during the weekend. If you want to reach a higher level you will need to study your own games after they are over, and for that you will need to keep a **score** of the moves. You will also benefit from playing through games by masters in chess books and magazines.

"CHESSPORT"

Chess is a universal passport, wherever you go you will meet people who are happy to play you, even if you cannot speak each other's languages. You can play almost anywhere – from giant-sized boards to floating boards in swimming pools!

Chess Literature

If you become serious you will want to read about the intricacies of the game. In old literature the moves may seem incomprehensible, as they are not in standard **notation**. Before there was an agreed standard, the moves were described. From a book written in 1614: "Imagine that the white King for his first draught playeth his owne pawne into the fourth house before himself, and the blacke King for his first draught playeth his Pawne in the like manner" – or 1 e4 e5.

Descriptive Notation

Over the years, shorter versions became established, and by the 19th century, the system initials were used. The initials of the man and the initial and number of the destination, gives **notation** such as 1 P-K4 P-K4, (pawn to king's fourth square for White, and Black). The drawbacks to the system are that each square has two names, one from White's side of the board and one from Black's, and it can be difficult to disentangle two like pieces moving to the same square.

Getting a Game

Progress depends on finding a range of stronger players, to meet a variety of styles. Players with a rich imagination can create a bewildering range of attacks, while there are those who play with the utmost precision. In time, your own personality will show in your games. Every great player began by losing hundreds of games, so chance your luck, and you will only learn from experience.

FAMOUS GAMES

Games that give enjoyment and instruction

ONCE YOU HAVE LEARNED to play correctly, much the best way of improving is to study games by masters. You will find these in newspapers and books. Conventionally, the names of the opposing players are shown either side of a hyphen, White-Black. At first you will need explanations, so look for games that are annotated, that is, with notes for the difficult moves. It will also help if **diagrams** are given. The games here are shorter than average, but offer plenty of entertainment as well as providing valuable instruction. All are from friendly play, with the exception of the first, which is from a master tournament played in 1950. When you find that you can play through games without error, you can concentrate on thinking about the player's ideas. Try covering up future moves and see if you can work them out first.

LEARNING FROM THE MASTERS
At first you might make mistakes in playing the moves from a printed **score**. A board with letters and numbers on will help you to reach the right position. Play through these games several times. You will find that the longer you give to their study, the more they yield in return.

KERES-ARLAMOWSKI

1 e4 c6 2 Nc3 d5 3 Nf3 dxe4
4 Nxe4 Nf6 5 Qe2 Nbd7 6
Nd6+ **mate**. Black, seeing
only a knight **exchange**,
overlooked that his e-pawn
would be **pinned** to the
king if the knight on e4
moved. He also blocked
the only square to which
the king could move.

NIGHT AT THE OPERA

Morphy played the Duke of Brunswick
and Count Isouard in Paris, 1858. This
is perhaps the most famous game. It
was played at the Paris Opera during
a performance of "The Barber of
Seville". The Duke and the Count
consulted each other before making
their joint move. Morphy, easily the
greatest player of his time, and an
opera lover, had to
sit with his back to
the stage during
the game. The
noblemen did not
make any gross
blunders. This
is the position
after Black's
12th move.

• **BLACK KNIGHT**
Morphy **sacrifices**
a white rook for this
black knight, enabling
his final **piece** to be
brought into play.
Although a rook
down, all White's
pieces are active.

• **ROOK**
Black's **king's-
side** rook and
bishop are never
brought into
the fray.

– MORPHY-DUKE OF BRUNSWICK & COUNT ISOUARD –

1 e4 e5 2 Nf3 d6 is the Philidor Defence.
3 d4 Bg4 is not ideal, but not a mistake. 4
dxe5 Bxf3 5 Qxf3 dxe5 6 Bc4 Nf6. Black
supposed they would be able to win back
their pawn. 7 Qb3 attacks the pawns on b7
and f7, 7...Qe7 8 Nc3 developing his knight,
is better than a pawn win. 8...c6 9 Bg5 b5
10 Nxb5 cxb5 11 Bxb5+ Nbd7 12 0-0-0.
Morphy's **pieces** are much more active
than those of his opponents. 12...Rd8 13

Rxd7 Rxd7 14 Rd1 Qe6 is an attempt to
unpin the knight, but the game is lost
here. 15 Bxd7+. An ordinary player would
continue 15 Qxe6+ fxe6 16 Bxf6 gxf6 17
Bxd7+ and grind out a win. Morphy shows
his genius by playing a move that allows a
recapture on d7 with the knight. 15...Nxd7
16 Qb8+. This queen **sacrifice** is obvious
– afterwards. Many would overlook it.
16...Nxb8 17 Rd8+ **mate**.

MOVES WITH A STING

This is from a game played in London, 1853. The board shows the position after White's 14th move. If one of your **pieces** is attacked, sometimes you can attack an enemy piece in return rather than move your own piece, as on White's sixth move.

• BISHOP
Black's strong bishop on f5 exerts a powerful effect on the **diagonal** b1-h7, leaving no legal move for White's king.

SCHULDER-BODEN

1 e4 e5 2 Nf3 d6, the Philidor Defence. 3 c3 f5 4 Bc4 Nf6 5 d4 fxe4 6 dxe5 exf3 7 exf6 Qxf6 8 gxf3, White's **king's-side** pawns are now weak – **isolated** and **doubled**. 8...Nc6 9 f4 to prevent 9...Ne5 attacking the bishop and also the pawn on f3. 9...Bd7 10 Be3 0-0-0 11 Nd2 Re8 12 Qf3 Bf5 13 0-0-0 d5 – a move with a sting! 14 Bxd5 Qxc3+ 15 bxc3 Ba3+ **mate**; this type is known as Boden's Mate.

18TH MOVE •
The bishop captures the rook on g1 as Black's reply to White's 18th move.

"THE IMMORTAL GAME"

"The Immortal Game", was played by Anderssen and Kieseritzky, in London, 1851. This is the position at the turning point of the game. If instead of Black's move 18...Bxg1, Black had played 18...Bxd6, then 19 Nxd6+ Kd8 20 Nxf7+ Ke8 21 Nd6+ Kd8 22 Qf8 **mate**. 18...Qxa1+ 19 Ke2 Qb2 would be a better idea.

ANDERSSEN-KIESERITZKY

1 e4 e5 2 f4 exf4. The King's Gambit is accepted. 3 Bc4 Qh4+ 4 Kf1 b5. Black hoped to deflect the bishop from f7, and make it possible to play his pawn to c6. 5 Bxb5 Nf6 6 Nf3 Qh6. Usually 6...Qh5 is played here, but Kieseritzky wanted to keep that square free for his knight. 7 d3 Nh5 8 Nh4. The threat of 8...Ng3+ **forking** king and rook was obvious, so it might have been better to develop the **pieces**. 8...Qg5 attacks two undefended pieces at the same time. 9 Nf5 c6 10 g4 Nf6 11 Rg1 cxb5 12 h4 Qg6 13 h5 Qg5 14 Qf3 threatens 15 Bxf4 to win the queen. Black's reply is the only way to avoid losing a piece. 14...Ng8 15 Bxf4 Qf6 16 Nc3 Bc5 16...Qe6 is better. 17 Nd5 Qxb2 18 Bd6 – a brilliant move. 18...Bxg1 19 e5 Qxa1+ 20 Ke2 Black **resigns**, because if 20...Na6 21 Nxg7+ Kd8 22 Qf6+ Nxf6 23 Be7 **mate**, or 20...Bb7 21 Nxg7+ Kd8 22 Qxf7 Nh6 23 Ne6+ dxe6 24 Qe7+ Kc8 25 Qc7 mate.

"THE EVERGREEN"

The following game is known as "The Evergreen". Anderssen played Dufresne in Berlin, 1852. After Morphy, Anderssen was the world's best player. White hopes to take advantage of the open **file** at the 19th move with Rad1, bringing us to this position. A modern Grandmaster, Fine, said this was probably the most profound concept seen in chess at that time.

BLACK QUEEN •
The queen threatens immediate **mate** after taking the knight on f3. All White's moves must **check**.

ANDERSSEN-DUFRESNE

1 e4 e5 2 Nf3 Nc6 3 Bc4 Bc5 4 b4 the Evans Gambit. 4...Bxb4 5 c3 Ba5 6 d4 exd4 White's c-pawn is **pinned**. 7 0-0 d3 The usual moves here are 7...d6 8 cxd4 or 7...dxc3 and White to recapture with the b1-knight; Dufresne wanted to make Nc3 difficult for White. 8 Qb3 Qf6 9 e5 Qg6. If 9...Nxe5 10 Re1 d6 11 Qb5+ costs Black a **piece**. 10 Re1 Nge7 11 Ba3 b5

sacrifices a pawn to get his pieces into action, and restrict Anderssen's queen. 12 Qxb5 Rb8 13 Qa4 Bb6. If 13...0-0, 14 Bxe7 and the c6-knight is **overloaded**. It cannot recapture on e7 without the bishop on a5 losing its guard. 14 Nbd2 Bb7 15 Ne4 Qf5 16 Bxd3 Qh5 17 Nf6+. The knight on e7 is **pinned** after the pawn recapture, 18 exf6. 17...gxf6 18 exf6 Rg8 19 Rad1.

MATING POSITION

When Anderssen made his 19th move he had to calculate precisely the rest of the game, and all possible variations. All the time Black was poised to play Qxg2 **mate** and so there was no breathing space – every move had to be a **check**.

ANDERSSEN'S MATING MOVES

FOUR BISHOPS •
Black's bishops are ideally placed for attack, but there is no time. White's bishops, assisted by a humble pawn, give **checkmate**.

19...Qxf3. Now Black is threatening immediate **mate** by capturing the **pinned** g-pawn with the queen. 20 Rxe7+ Nxe7. If 20...Kf8 then 21 Re3+ discovered **check** wins the queen. If 20...Kd8, 21

Rxd7+ Kc8 22 Rd8+ Nxd8 23 Qd7+ Kxd7 24 Bf5+ Ke8 25 Bd7 mate. 21 Qxd7+ Kxd7 22 Bf5+. The powerful double check. Black plays 22...Ke8 as 22...Kc6 then 23 Bd7 mate. 23 Bd7+ Kf8 24 Bxe7+ mate.

CHESS DIVERSIONS

Now that you've finished, here's where you begin!

MOST CHESS ACTIVITY is between two players in the home or at a club. You can find out about these from your local information service in your library, neighborhood newspaper, or district leisure department. Your national chess body will be also be able to provide you with details of chess clubs. There are many books on chess, as well as a wide range of quality periodicals. You can even examine foreign magazines because standard **notation** is international. In this way, chess can help you to learn another language.

POSTAL CHESS

For many players, especially those with physical handicaps, unsocial working hours, living in remote areas, or having limited free time, correspondence chess provides a means of playing the game from home. The players work out their moves and then send them to their opponent by post, phone, fax, or telex. The standard of play can be high, because players can try out ideas on a board and test their moves with a computer to avoid major blunders.

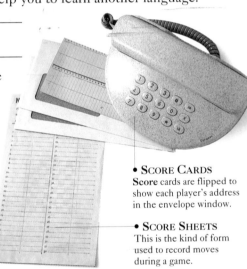

• **SCORE CARDS**
Score cards are flipped to show each player's address in the envelope window.

• **SCORE SHEETS**
This is the kind of form used to record moves during a game.

Juniors playing on the top of a bus

COMPETITIVE CHESS

Once you are playing confidently, you might like to try your skill in a match or a tournament. Play can be at many levels. You may wish to join your local chess club, or perhaps take part in something less formal in a pub or café, where chess is played. Tournaments take place regularly all over the world, often with hundreds of competitors in different events, like this one shown left, according to their skills.

PROBLEMS

A **problem** is a composed position that usually bears a stipulation such as "White to move and **mate** in two moves". It is usually clear that White has an easy win, the difficulty lies in meeting the artificial demand to do it in the number of moves specified. Normal chess criteria do not apply, so working on problems does not help to improve playing strength, but you will get practice in working out moves.

PROBLEM

This **problem** is by John Rice, first published in *The Problemist* magazine, in 1982. White is to move and **mate** in two moves against any defense. The key move is 1 Rb6.

Much of the joy of problems lies in working out why every man there is essential to the composition, and why other moves fail. The chess problem world is an independent area. Once they succumb to its spell, many chess enthusiasts give up playing in its favor.

COLLECTING

There are some related activities for which you need not even touch your chessmen! Most of them have their own associations. For example, there are stamp, book, and set collectors.

• **POSTCARDS**
Postcards and a "First Day" Cover showing chess themes.

STAMPS •
There have been around 300 chess stamps produced.

STUDIES

Some chessplayers take up **studies**. Like **problems**, these are composed positions, usually **endgame**. There is no demand to mate in "x" moves. The task is to find either a win or a draw from positions that appear to be drawn or lost respectively. Although the positions are uncommon, the usual considerations of play apply, and practicing them can improve skill. This one is by Emanuel Lasker, 1890.

STUDY BOARD

White can force a draw easily, but how to win? 1 Kb7 Rb2+ 2 Ka7 Rc2 3 Rh5+ Ka4 4 Kb7 Rb2+ 5 Ka6 Rc2 6 Rh4+ Ka3 7 Kb6 Rb2+ 8 Ka5 Rc2 9 Rh3+ Ka2. The surprise move is 10 Rxh2 Rxh2 11 c8=Q with a clear win.

COLLECTING SETS

Although few decorative sets are of significance in chess history, or are suitable for play, they can be a delight purely for their elegance and diversity.

French king

Muslim knight

Tyrolean "bishop"

German rook

GLOSSARY

Words in *italic* are glossary entries.

A

- **Array** The position of the chessmen on the board before the game begins.

B

- **Back rank** The *rank* nearest the player, from which the *pieces* begin.
- **Backward pawn** A pawn that has no allied pawn level with or behind it on an adjacent *file*, that can ever defend it.

C

- **Castle** A special move of the king, involving the simultaneous movement of two *pieces* – the rook and the king.
- **Check** An attack on a king, from which it may, or may not, escape.
- **Checkmate** A situation in which a king is in *check*, and cannot escape.
- **Close game** One that begins 1 d4.
- **Combination** A series of tactical devices strung together as part of a concerted plan, often with a *sacrifice*.

D

- **Diagonal** An oblique sequence of squares, connected at their corners.
- **Diagram** A conventional two-dimensional representation of the board and the men, used in chess literature.
- **Double attack** A simultaneous attack on two different targets.
- **Doubled pawns** Two pawns of the same color on the same *file*, usually regarded as a weakness.
- **Doubled rooks** Two rooks of the same color mutually supporting each other on the same *rank* or *file*, usually a strength.

A pawn marked with string may be used on promotion to a piece

E

- **Endgame** The final phase of the game when few men are left on the board.
- **Ending** A *study* – to some extent the terms *endgame* and ending are interchangeable, but a study is not necessarily the end of a game.
- **En passant** A special capturing possibility available to a pawn where an opponent's pawn uses the initial double-move facility to bypass attack.
- **Exchange** This has two meanings. An exchange is simply a swap. To win (or lose) a rook for a *minor piece* is to win (or lose) the exchange.

F

- **File** A straight row of squares going from one player to their opponent.
- **Forced move** A move for which there is no alternative, or no sensible one.
- **Fool's Mate** The shortest possible game ending in *mate*. It seldom happens because White's second move is pointless. 1 f4 e6 2 g4 Qh4+ mate.
- **Fork** A simultaneous attack on two men by one *piece*, although the term is often restricted to describing such attacks by either a knight or a pawn.

H

- **Half-open file** A *file* on which only one player has a pawn or pawns.
- **Half-passed pawn** A pawn on a *half-open file* that can, with the help of an allied pawn, become a *passed pawn*.
- **Hole** A square that cannot be defended by a pawn but can be occupied by an enemy *piece*. This may be a weakness.

I

- **Isolated pawn** A pawn with no allied pawn on either of the adjacent *files*.

J

- **J'adoube** A largely obsolete French phrase, often used when a player adjusts a man. Any words or phrase will do to meet the laws of chess so long as the player makes it clear the intention is to tidy the board rather than make a move.

K

• **King's side** The *files* f, g, and h, and sometimes the e-file is included also.

M

• **Major piece** Queen or rook.
• **Mate** Abbreviation for *checkmate*.
• **Material** All the *pieces* and pawns on the board, apart from the king.
• **Middlegame** The phase of the game between *opening* and *endgame*.
• **Minor piece** A bishop or a knight.

N

• **Notation** Method of recording the moves of a game – the *score*.

O

• **Open file** One with no pawns on it.
• **Open game** A game beginning 1 e4 e5.
• **Opening** The first phase of the game, often utilizing moves already known from previous games.
• **Outpost** A favorable square in the enemy half of the board that can be occupied by a *piece* but cannot be attacked by a pawn. One player's *hole* is another player's outpost.
• **Overload** Giving a *piece* too many tasks, e.g. defending two men at once.
• **Overprotection** A deliberate defense of a key point by more force than is absolutely necessary.

P

• **Passed pawn** A pawn with no enemy pawn in front of it on its own or either of the adjacent *files*.
• **Perpetual check** A series of unstoppable *checks* that usually lead to a draw by threefold repetition of position, often made to avoid a loss.
• **Piece** King, queen, bishop, knight, or rook. A pawn is not a piece.
• **Pin** An attack by a line *piece* on a man which is unable, or appears to be unable, to move without putting its king in *check*, or exposing to capture a valuable piece that is sheltered.
• **Problem** A composed position for solving to which the normal laws of chess do not apply (compare *study*).
• **Promotion** The substitution of a queen, knight, rook, or bishop, of the same color, for a pawn that has reached the enemy's *back rank*, on the same move.

Q

• **Queen** To *promote* a pawn to a queen.
• **Queen's side** The a-, b-, and c-*files*, and sometimes also the d-file.

R

• **Rank** A row of alternate-colored squares going left to right (or vice versa) from a player's viewpoint.
• **Resign** To give up the game.

S

• **Sacrifice** To give up *material*, sometimes temporarily, in order to attack, or to fend off an attack.
• **Scholar's Mate** This can occur quite often between beginners, with slight differences in moves sometimes, 1 e4 e5 2 Bc4 Bc4 3 Qh5 Nc6 4 Qxf7+ *mate*. The correct response for Black would have been 3...Qe7, defending the pawn and preventing mate.
• **Score** The written record of the moves of a game, usually on a score sheet.
• **Seventh rank** The *rank* on which the enemy's pawns stand at the *array*.
• **Skewer** An attack by a line *piece* on a more valuable enemy piece which must then move, exposing to capture another man on the same line.
• **Stalemate** A position in which a king is not in *check* but the player has no legal move. Such a position is a draw.
• **Study** A composed position that observes the normal laws of chess.

U

• **Underpromotion** *Promotion* to a rook, knight, or bishop, as an alternative to promoting the pawn to a queen.
• **United pawns** Pawns on adjoining *files* that are capable of supporting each other.

An inverted rook is often used to show a pawn on its promotion

INDEX

GETTING IN TOUCH

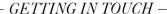

Manhattan Chess Club
154 West 57th Street
New York
NY 10019
Tel: 212-333-5888

US Chess Federation
186 Route 9W
New Windsor, New York
12553-7698
Tel: 914-562-8350

ACKNOWLEDGMENTS

Ken Whyld and Dorling Kindersley would like to thank the following for their help in the production of this book:

Jane Johnson, Cathy Forbes, and Rodney Forte for modeling. Eureka Electronics, Brighton, for loan of the Novag computer, and Countrywide Computers, Wilburton, Cambs, for loan of the Mephisto computer. BT Phoneshop, London W1, for loan of the telephone.

Richard Blakey for producing the model chessboard. Gareth Williams for allowing us access to his private chess collection. Hamleys, London, for their advice, and hire of Crown Staunton chessmen. Broadgate Estates plc, London, for permission to photograph their outdoor chess set on location.

Schiller quotation (p.18) from *Day's Collacon: An Encyclopædia of Prose Quotations*. Problem (p.91) by John Rice, published in *The Problemist* 1982. Study (p.91) by Emanuel Lasker, 1890.

Philip Gatward, photographer, and his assistant, Dean Belcher. Rodney Forte for photography assistance on location shots. Emma Kotch for hair and make-up. Sarah Larter and Tony Mudd for editorial assistance, Sam Grimmer for design assistance, and Hilary Bird for the index. Janos Marffy for line drawings, Liz Wheeler for computer artworks. Mark Huba for the use of chess tournament photograph (p.90*bl*).